ACKNOWLEDGMENTS

Dedicated to Dr. Daisy Osborn
a pioneer

Our gratitude and thanks to the following people who helped with the various stages of this workbook:

Gayretta Beckrum
Evelyn Jiffron
Charlotte Lemons
Barb Rarden
Annyce Stone

INTRODUCTION

The reconciliation of men and women to the Divine purposes of God is the reestablishment of a creational law. Man and woman were created in the image of God as His vice-regents in the earth to establish civilization and government. The Scriptures clearly established that the man and the woman were co-essential, co-substantial and co-equal. They were to co-labor together in accomplishing this Divine mandate.

Human rebellion and the violation of Divine law brought about a breach of the creational covenant. The consequences of such human failure resulted in the introduction of sin into the creational order, a violation of the creational initiative and a distortion of the male and female relationship.

However, redemption was the assumption of the original Divine intention. What the first Adam forfeited, the Second Adam, Christ Jesus, recovered. And now the benefits of redemption are available to the created order. Yet, this understanding has not been fully appropriated in historical writings and various scholarly treatments of the Genesis story. Consequently, distortions of the male and female relationship have been perpetuated in the family, society and the Church.

Redemptive equality must be given its full expression theologically and practically. The true meaning of the term is often modified when such issues as government and function are discussed. The phrase "in Christ" carries tremendous redemptive significance when attached to issues of sex, race, and socioeconomic categories. However, the concept does not eliminate the natural distinctions of such groups. Although redemption is the "equalizer" and provides access to Divine privileges and rights regardless of sex, financial status, age, or race, it does not change "the leopards' spots nor the Ethiopian's skin." For in the world the physical and reproductive differences between men and women still remain. In the economy of life, the poor and the elderly still struggle with the issues of money and aging. The physical distinctions may still exist between racial groupings. But the legal fact of redemption eliminates the prohibitions of rights, opportunities, and governmental functions placed upon anyone because of gender, socioeconomic status, race, and age.

The intended objectives of this study is to research the Scriptures, the historical and contemporary writings that have influenced the prevalent attitudes toward women and their relationship with men in the culture. In the process, we will endeavor to maintain the proper relationship of our topic with God's overall concern and rule for the created order. Any topic of research that loses its perspective with God's overall kingdom agenda will ultimately falter on the steps of intellectuality and humanistic reasoning. The emphasis here will be simple: to rediscover the initial co-laborship function and to revalidate the creational premise that **God gave them.**

FOREWORD

The treatment of any topic, whether Biblical, social, political or ideological, must begin with a clear understanding of the sovereignty of God as expressed in creation and in the ordering of all things. The book of Genesis is preparatory to all Divine revelation of God as Creator and Ruler. If our perception about Genesis is incorrect, then the magnitude of our error will be pronounced in our treatment of the New Testament Scriptures.

If we accept the Scriptures as "inspired" and "inerrant", then we must accept them as a record of revelation of Divine activity. For purposes of clarity, "inerrancy" does not stake its claim on "literalism" at the expense of figurative interpretation. "Inerrancy" does not disregard the issues of context, culture and objectivity of the Scriptures. To the contrary, "inerrancy" takes into account the Divine and human element in the recording of Scriptures without "wrestling" over alleged contradictions in the Scriptures.

In our approach to this topic, we felt it absolutely necessary to emphasize the preeminence of God and His kingdom. This topic, like any other, must be treated in its relationship with God's overall revelation and not as an isolated subject. We must ultimately move **beyond gender** to the ultimate issues of Jesus Christ and things concerning the Kingdom of God.

A. Creation was a Divine, unilateral and unassisted action of the supreme authority of God.

B. Creation begins with the authority of God. This is an expression of the sovereignty or the preeminence of Divine rule in establishing the beginning of all things. God is sovereign in creation, organization and in the maintenance of the created order. God is the source of all authority.

C. The world and all animate and inanimate things have their origin in God. They are not self-existent nor did they evolve from existing things. God created all things (*bara*, created something out of nothing.)

D. The amount of time of the creational process is not stated, and the order of creational events is not given any hierarchal significance. That is, the events of the first day were not stated to be more important than the events of subsequent days.

E. Mankind, male and female, are created beings and morally responsible to God. The relationship between God and mankind is more than a Creator/creature relationship. The relationship is **governmental**. God instructed them to rule and He established the parameters of their responsibility. Mankind, therefore, was made morally responsible to God. This is the origin of the concept of covenant, delegated authority, and government.

F. The human creatures, male and female, were and still are made in the image of God and are distinct from the animals. The "image of God" speaks of Divine capacities imparted to these created beings and may have included the following:

1. Rationality — the gift of intelligence and power to reason, communicate and plan.

2. Creativity — the capacity to make things and impart value to them.

3. Dominion — the mastery over created things; control over the environment; harnessing and managing the forces of nature; and the capacity to create culture and civilization.

4. Righteousness — the capacity to know the revealed will of God and to impart Divine preferences and values where life is concerned.

5. Community — the capacity to live together in life relationships.

G. Mankind was not constituted to sin, but was constituted intellectually and psychologically to live in righteousness. Sin was a contradiction to the nature of these created beings. However, rationality provides the capacity for communication, commission, and conduct. It also created the possibility to sin or to act irrationally. Hence, mankind's original righteousness was not irrefutable. The protection of humanity rested in their obedience and communion with God.

H. The rule and government of God is evident in creation and in the delegation of authority to the man and woman. The creation of Adam (male/female) was proceeded by a commandment. The parameters of human authority were clearly established. They were to be vice-reagents of Divine authority. The relationship between the man and the woman was one of equality governmentally, although distinctively different reproductively.

I. Disobedience of humanity to Divine authority introduces disorganization and disorder into the created order. This entrance of evil into the created order causes an 'unsettledness', a separation, negation, disruption, and disharmony. This sin is a progressive disorientation.

J. The cause of this sin and rebellion along with the implication of the woman, man, and the serpent will be addressed fully in the next section. The Divine response to human failure is seen in restoration, redemption, restructuring, and regeneration. There is the restoration of divine purposes and government; the intervention of God into human affairs; and the formation of a *prophetic community* in which the human response to Divine law can be activated through the establishment of relationships, laws, and standards.

K. The implication of the Genesis account on the New Testament revelation will be reflective in the issue of gender in government, society, and the Church.

CONTENTS

THE DYNAMICS OF CHANGE

My son and I were discussing the relocation of his family to New York. He is an attorney, and his wife had been accepted to medical school. This required a significant change in their lives. As we dialogued about the relocation process, we created a list of the new things that would be the result of this move, including a house, community, church, friends, healthcare, shopping areas, transportation, and day care. This move to New York represented a comprehensive event that involved all of the family members and every aspect of their lives. It was a significant change.

Life is a series of changes. These changes are not limited to geographical and occupational moves, but may also be informational or even relational. New information, ideas, options, and even people are constantly being presented to us by our environment. Age, marriage, children, divorce, health challenges, death, education, new friends and associates present new options and opportunities to us as well. The process by which we respond to this disruption of our status quo is called transition. Because we are rational creatures, change evokes emotional and even physical responses from us. Since we must constantly experience this ongoing variation in our environment and the information that it provides us, the effective management of our individual transitions becomes a goal for us all. There is no way around this. Every one of us will experience this disruptive event called change. The difference will rest in the management of the transition process and this is within our control.

In this section, we will learn to view the dynamics of change as a *beneficial crisis* and the different phases involved in processing change events as new information and options are presented.

Two Categories of People

We normally encounter two categories of people as we teach on this topic: the **learned** and the **unlearned**. The unlearned individuals suffer only from a deficit of information and knowledge. They find the information to change less difficult because they have very few roots to pull up and virtually no landmarks to move. Unlearned individuals have very few convictions and tend to accept new information and ideas readily because the information does not conflict with their current belief system. The learned individuals are those who have many convictions. Over time they have assimilated much information. Not all they have been taught is true, unfortunately, but the clash of new information may result in rejection when it does not coincide with their current belief system. Will Rogers said, "It ain't what we know that hurts us. It's what we know that ain't so." The rate of transition varies between these two groups in part because of the level of previous awareness of information and the amount of time certain belief systems have been operational.

Positioning Change

Let's state at the outset that the introduction of new ideas and information does not require the rejection of existing knowledge. Contemporary thought is not always the enemy of historic foundations. New truth does not always annihilate old truth. Foundations are at times reinforced by the scaffolding of new information and ideas.

So new information must be put in a proper context with old information. There must be the establishment of the relationship that exists between that which is known and that which is now being made available to us. Henry Ford first introduced the Model T automobile as a basic method of transportation. It rivaled the horse and buggy, but it did not provide much passenger comfort. With time, competition from other automobile manufacturers and the desire of the public for more comfort, Henry Ford introduced a new, more comfortable model but it was still built upon the foundation of the old Model T. New technology was placed in proper relation with the old. Thus, when "new" revelation and understanding of God's Word arises, we must place it in proper relation with the old.

The Three Phases of the Journey

When people are introduced to something new, they begin a process of assimilation, which may illicit a variety of emotions. People who have invested a lot of time and energy in the status quo will probably experience an emotional struggle as they work their way through the transition process. The three phases of the journey are described as omega, discovery and alpha. Each of these phases is portrayed in part by a variety of emotions. We shall discuss them in some detail.

1. **Omega**. This is a time of ending or finalizing existing thoughts and information. The key focus during this phase is loss, of that which is going away and being given up upon the introduction of something new. The shock of new ideas, information and patterns varies based upon the receiver (learned and unlearned) and the context in which the new is placed in relationship to the old (complementary or contradictory). The unlearned group generally has no basis of comparison between what they know and what is being introduced to them; therefore, the new elements are neither complementary nor contradictory. This group meets the new with less negative energy and emotions because there is an absence of conflict. The learned group, on the other hand, may well react to the shock with a greater variety of emotional responses because there is generally a disruption of prevalent belief or value system. Of course the context in which the old and the new are placed will

greatly influence the impact of the disruption. The behavior exhibited can be described as follows:

➢ **denial** - this is not true; it does not work; I cannot believe this!

➢ **anger** - don't mess with my mind; stop confusing me; I don't like what I'm hearing!

➢ **anxiety** - I don't know if this will work; I can't believe this is true!

➢ **confusion** - I don't understand; I don't know what to do!

➢ **resignation** - I quit; I give up; I want to leave right now!

Of course new information may also be greeted with relief and enthusiasm. When old information had been disturbing, the reaction to new may well be "Thank God! I always hoped there was another way to look at this"! The introduction of some new elements may also create "shock waves" which are totally unrelated to the topic of discussion. For example, an individual in the midst of a personal crisis may display a disproportionate emotional response to a very minor challenge to their current belief system. In fact, the matter being discussed or introduced at the moment may be totally unrelated to the response being generated. I was teaching a seminar when I noticed that several of the members of the audience began to fold their arms and display painful expressions on their faces. At first, I thought their responses were related to the material I had just introduced, or perhaps my delivery of the information. However, during a break in the seminar I discussed their response with our host. She informed me that those individuals all worked for the same organization, and had just recently gone through a very disruptive series of events. During my presentation, I had shared a seemingly harmless example of an employer/employee relationship, and it was a duplication of the very crisis they had all encountered. Their response during the seminar was not antagonistic to the material but to the memory of a historical event, which was stimulated by presentation. It is important to understand that people may be at various stages of transitions involving many different events in their personal lives. Their responses during the introduction of new information or patterns may be totally unrelated to the new elements.

New information, ideas and patterns have the proven ability to provoke such emotions. The depth of the emotions depends upon the personality dynamics of the individual, the amount of time already invested in the prevalent belief system, and the degree of conflict produced by the disruption of the status quo.

All this is provided simply to say the emotions of change should not be condemned nor denied. People are rational creatures and often engage the full dimension of their psychophysical beings in the process of change. They should be allowed to express their emotions and the nature of their response, be it conflict or agreement, which is generated by the introduction of new elements into their hearts and minds. However, it is possible and even necessary to move beyond this phase in order to explore the possibility of integrating the new elements with their current beliefs.

It is important to help people understand this omega phase of change and their various emotional responses. As teachers and instructors, we should avoid offering simplistic solutions to the complexity of human responses. When we properly discern the phases of the change process we can insure a proper interpretation of the reactions of people during the introduction of new elements into their existing information mix and respond effectively.

2. **Discovery**. Once new elements have been introduced into the knowledge pool, there follows a period of investigation. During this phase the individual begins to explore the possibility of accepting and integrating new elements. During this stage, there is a need for information and dialogue. There needs to be the

presentation of various models, options and ways to assimilate new elements into the existing belief system.

There are a variety of emotional responses during this phase:

> **frustration** - What do I do with what I already know?

> **conflict** - It does not fit together

> **realization of loss** - I have believed this so long!

> **approach - avoidance**- I believe it but I need time to put it together!

> **confusion** - Do I have to discard everything! I don't understand!

Our response at this phase should be one of openness and patience. Questions asked deserve our respectful answers. Defensiveness will harm the process and the participants. It's important to recognize that resistance is <u>not</u> a rejection of the ideas, it's an expression of discomfort about the change.

3. **Alpha.** This phase is best described as integration and application. The individuals who have moved successfully into this alpha phase generally comprehend the new stuff! In fact, they become so enthusiastic that they want to go out and introduce other people to it. Some of the emotions that are exhibited are as follows:

> **real enthusiasm** - this is great; let's go tell others!

> **trust** - I believe it!

> **relief/anxiety** – I am glad it is over! I am now clear about how this is going to affect me!

> **enthusiasm** - I am excited about this! What else can I learn?

> **hopeful/skeptical** - I believe, but help my unbelief!
>   I understand how it works, but will my friends?

Conclusion

There are several facts that seem to be consistent when engaging people with new material.

1. People need to feel that they are understood and validated when going through the phases of change. (Validation moves people out of Omega)

2. Information and communication are necessary at every level of change. (This moves people to Alpha)

3. Even when people are rewarded and given incentives to change, they will still experience feelings of loss.

4. The longer a group or an individual has accepted a certain belief system, the greater the resistance and the reaction to change.

5. Reactions are not always a result of the information being presented.

6. Transitions can be multiple, and people can be at various stages of an omega experience at the same time.

7. Emotional reactions are at least as important as any other aspect of implementing change.

As you are introduced to some new information in this document, be aware of the dynamics of change. Allow yourself to experience the various phases of transition. And remember that new information does

not always require the rejection of existing belief systems. Let us place new information and ideas in the proper context with our existing information pool.

Note: Barb Rarden, Clarion Consultants, taught this at our first seminar and has graciously granted permission to include the above concepts in our book.

2

THE GENESIS STORY

Scriptural Reference: Genesis 1-3

Genesis is the only Divinely inspired record of creational intentions and purposes.

1. The creation of mankind is clearly stated in the text: *Let Us make man in Our image, according to Our likeness;* **let them** *have dominion over the fish of the sea, over the birds of the air, and over the cattle, over all the earth and over every creeping thing that creeps on the earth. (Genesis 1:26)*

    The designation of *man* here is not *gender* specific but includes male and female. The text clearly records that *He created him; male and female He created them.*

2. A distinction must be made between creation and formation. **Creation** is to bring forth something out of nothing. There are no ingredients and no mixing instructions. What is created did not previously exist. **Formation** is a post-creation process and takes advantage of something that already exists. To form is to refine, to polish, to shape and to sculpture for a particular purpose. God created the heavens and the earth and He *formed man of the dust of the ground, and breathed into his nostrils the breath of life and man became a living being. (Genesis 2:7,8)*, (Isaiah 45:18)

---

3. God gave His newly created humanity five commands: *Be fruitful and multiply; fill the earth and subdue it; have dominion over the fish of the sea, over the birds of the air, and over every living thing that moves on the earth.* (Genesis 1:28)

The commands were to be fruitful, multiply, replenish the earth, subdue it and have dominion. It is important to note that the commission was given to them, **both male and female.**

Now the text gets specific with the detail of the duties of these vice-reagents of the planet:

> *Then the Lord God took the man and put him in the garden of Eden to tend and keep it. And the Lord God commanded the man, saying, "Of every tree of the garden you may freely eat; but of the tree of the knowledge of good and evil you shall not eat, for in the day that you eat of it you shall surely die." (Genesis 2:15-17)*

To "tend" is an agricultural term meaning to develop and cultivate. To "keep" is used in a militaristic context meaning to guard and protect. Dominion means to make something productive and to guard against its destruction.

4. The text does not give a definite time before a Divine observation is made:

> *And the Lord God said, it is not good that man should be alone; I will make him a helper comparable to him. (Genesis 2:18)*

The word "alone" in the Hebrew means "in his separation"and is not to be confused with contemporary meaning of "singular" or "by himself." It implies that Adam, the man, was drifting apart from God. The word "help" comes from the Hebrew word meaning "superior" or "same." This same term is used twenty-one times in the Old Testament with sixteen of these referring to "divine help" as in Psalm 121:1,2.

5. The formation of the woman out of the man is described in Genesis 2:22:

> *Then the rib which the Lord God had taken from the man He made into a woman, and He brought her to the man.*

The word "rib" in some translations means "side" or "chamber." The original Hebrew word *pleura* is properly translated in Daniel 7:5 and is used forty-two times in the Old Testament. It is only translated "rib" in the Genesis account of the woman. The word "rib" has been the motive behind the subordination of womanhood. Adam's response to this new creation called woman is quite clear: *This is now bone of my bone and flesh of my flesh; She shall be called woman, because she was taken out of man.*

Now a Divine declaration is made concerning the man and the woman and their families: *therefore a man shall leave his father and mother and be joined to his wife, and they shall become one flesh.*

6. The deception of the woman is now addressed. The text does not state the duration of time before the woman is recorded speaking to the serpent. Until this event occurs, the man and the woman are both sinless creatures with no guile nor iniquity. They are not devious, malicious, or rebellious creatures. They are both rational and capable of making decisions. The dialogue between the woman and the serpent is recorded in Genesis 3:1-6. *Now the serpent was more crafty than any of the wild animals the Lord God had made. He said to the woman, "Did God really say, 'You must not eat from any tree in the garden?"*

The woman said to the serpent, 'We may eat fruit from the trees in the garden, but God did say, 'You must not eat fruit from the tree that is in the middle of the garden, and you must not touch it, or you will die.' "

"You will not surely die," the serpent said to the woman. "For God

knows that when you eat of it your eyes will be opened, and you will be like God, knowing good and evil."

When the woman saw that the fruit of the tree was good for food and pleasing to the eye, and also desirable for gaining wisdom, she took some and ate it. She also gave some to her husband, who was with her, and he ate it.

The text does not record why the woman spoke to the serpent nor does it exclude the possibility that the man may have previously dialogued with the serpent. It is clear from the text that the serpent was "more cunning than any other beast."

No explanation is given of the motive behind Eve's sin. It is recorded that she did eat the fruit and that she gave some to Adam and he did eat. It is unwarranted speculation to conclude that the woman deceived or seduced the man into eating. The text offers no support to such a speculation. It is interesting that the first appearance of the word "covering" is in connection with sin.

7. The man and the woman respond to Divine inquiry. Adam responds in a manner that indicts God. Genesis 3:12 *The man said, The woman you put here with me - she gave me some fruit from the tree, and I ate it.* Adam does not assume any direct responsibility in the matter, nor does he mention the dialogue that occurred between the woman and the serpent. However, his response is an accurate one. The woman's response to Divine inquiry is accurate <u>and</u> perceptive: *The serpent deceived me, and I ate* (v.13). To be deceived is to believe a lie. It is to be persuaded against all other arguments or facts that the proposition presented is truth.

8. The consequences of disobedience are now discussed. The Lord acknowledges that the serpent did deceive the woman and He decrees judgment: *And the Lord said to the serpent: because you have done this, you are cursed more than all cattle, and more than every beast of the field; on your belly you shall go, and you shall eat dust all the days*

of your life. And I will put enmity between you and the woman, and between your seed and her Seed; He shall bruise your head, and you shall bruise His heal. (Genesis 3:14-15).

At this moment, God and the woman become allies against the serpent. The eschatological implications here are enormous. **The seed of the woman is Christ**. The prophetic declaration of war is made. Satan is now set to destroy the woman and her seed (Rev. 12:1-9). In the process, the woman becomes a friend of God in the war over her seed to destroy the works of the serpent. Jesus later acknowledged that He came to destroy the works of the Devil.

The response of God to the woman has been a source of much speculation: *To the woman He said: I will greatly multiply your sorrow and your conception; in pain you shall bring forth children; your desire shall be for your husband, and he shall rule over you. (Genesis 3:16).* The phrase, *your desire shall be for your husband,* is translated a little differently in the original text: *A snare has caused you sorrow and sighing; you shall turn toward your husband and he will rule over you.* The word "desire" was substituted in the original text in the sixteenth century by a Dominican monk named Pagnino. This mistranslation has led many to associate lustfulness to this passage and, consequently, to women. Also, in the original text, it is not a command for the man to rule over the woman, but Divine foreknowledge of the consequences of the woman turning from God and towards her husband. The original text seems to present this much disputed issue as a Divine word of knowledge, rather than a prophetic decree.

The woman was never cursed. Let us examine the text:

Then to Adam He said, "Because you have heeded the voice of your wife, and eaten from the tree of which I commanded you, saying, 'You shall not eat of eat of it,' cursed is the ground for your sakes; in toil shall you eat of it all the days of your life. Both thorns and thistles it shall bring forth for you, and you shall eat the herb of the field. In the sweat of your face you shall eat bread till you return to the ground, for out of it you were taken; for dust you are, and to dust you shall return.' (Genesis 3:17-19)

The serpent and the ground have been cursed but there is no indication that the woman was cursed. A faulty speculation of this point has been the basis of much gender bashing. The man and the woman both suffered the consequences of their disobedience. Neither of them was cursed. *The man was driven from the garden and the woman did follow him. (Genesis 3:23-24)*

The Genesis Story

WORD STUDY

Adonai	The Eternal self-existent God who is the author of all existence. The Eternal ADONAI (LORD) describes the Deity stressing HIS loving kindness, HIS acts of mercy, condescension and revelation to mankind
Alone	"In his separation," not single or by himself
Brethren	In the New Testament is *adelphio* (from the same womb) which without further qualifications usually means brothers and sisters
Deception	You believe a lie. The devil uses this to get you out of the position God gave you. Satan uses this to move mankind out of God's position of dominion.
Deceived	As in I Timothy 2:14 the Greek word *apato*, cheated, deluded, mislead in mind and judgment
Desire	Mistranslation by Pagnino. Original test says teshuqa. "You shall turn toward your husband..."
Dominion	The Hebrew word is *radah* and it means to tread down, subjugate; prevail against, reign, bear rule, rule over, take, dominate.
Elohim	The pluralistic GOD, GOD the Father, GOD the Son, and GOD the Holy Spirit. This is the more general divine name of GOD. ELOHIM (GOD) emphasizes His justice and rulership. God the creator, the universal GOD.
Enmity	The Hebrew word *eybah* meaning hostility, hatred, adversity, the oppression by one who seeks to injure and delights in accomplishment of it or the pursuit of hostility.
Equal	In scripture means to have value, access and opportunity.

WORD STUDY

Formation	A process that is in addition to creation; to form, refine or shape. (Isaiah 45:18)
Help, Helpmeet	Ezer, *negeb* - Hebrew words for helpmeet; old English "surrour" - to aid. Same as one superior to; face-to-face. Psalms 121:1-2 - helper as in Divine help.
Hupotassomenio	Submitting - voluntarily putting oneself under the other, applying to all.
Image	In the Hebrew is *tselm* which means representative or something cut out
Ish	A notable man of high degree
Ishna	A notable woman of high degree
Keep	Guard and protect, militaristic
Likeness	In Hebrew is demwuth which means resemblance, fashion
Man/mankind	The creation called man-humankind
Poimen	*The person (male/female*
Presbyteros	*Denotes a form of government*
Presbyter	The office
Prophet	One who speaks the heart of God for a nation, individual, or group
Rib	Pleura - side or chamber
Sons	Used in scripture to denote value or importance
Tend	Develop and cultivate, agriculture

DISCUSSION

1. Is there any hierarchical significance in the order of creation? Does the appearance of the man first have any governmental significance?

   The order of creation has been used as argument for the subordination of the woman to the man. There is no such position inferred in the text. If the order of creational or formational entities had some significance beacuse of their chronology, then the logical conclusion would be to give preeminence to the earth and the other living creatures. It is also alleged that the last event in a cycle of divine activity has governmental significance. However, neither of these conclusions seems valid in this instance.

2. Was the concept of dominion given to the man over the woman?

   Genesis 1:26-27 records the divine mandate. There is no gender specific reference attached to dominion. It seems logical, since there is no obvious reference to the contrary, that mandate was given to the man and the woman and that they were both to be God's vice-reagents.

3. Was there a divine decree subordinating the woman to the man? Was male dominance a consequence of the curse?

   The issue at state is found in Genesis 3:16 *To the woman, He said, "I will greatly multiply your sorrows and your conception, and in pain you shall bring forth children; your desire shall be for yourhusband and he shall rule over you"*. Dr. Moffitt's translation records it slightly differently: *To the woman he said, "I will make child-birth a sore pain for you, you shall have pangs in bearing; yet you shall crave to have your husbvand, and he shall master you"*. Dr. Bushnell gives yet another rendering of the last part of this passage: *Thou are turning away to thy husband, and he will rule over thee.* The word in question is "turning" or *tesuqa* in the Septuagint. It signifies "to turn away" and represents a volitional act on the part of the woman. It represents divine foreknowledge of the consequences of such a voluntary act.

4. Was Eve cursed?

No! Examine the text. God cursed two things; the serpent and the ground.

5. What prompted the creation of Eve?

Whatever God does is to be found within Himself. Unless He epecifically states the motive behind His action, it is simply speculation on our part. After the formation of Adam and his placement in the garden, there is no indication of the amount of time that lapsed before the creation of Eve. The divine observation is summed up in the words; *It is not good for man to be alone.* The Hebrew expression for "one alone" in Joshua 22:20 and Isaiah 51:2 seems more appropriate here, according to Dr. Bushnell. This expression means "in his separation."

Dr. Alexander Whyte in his book, *Bible Characters*, records the possibility of something in the nature of a stumble in Adam while yet alone in the garden. Eve was created to 'help' Adam recover himself, and to establish himself in the garden, and in the favor, fellowship and service of God.

6. What is the meaning of the phrase "help meet?"

The word "help" does not imply an inferior, but a superior help. The word "meet" denotes "face-to-face." The word appears frequently in the Old Testament and is used twice of Eve. With few exceptions (Isaiah 30:5, Ezekiel 12:14, and Daniel 11:34), the word refers to divine help, as in Psalm 121:2, *My help cometh from the Lord.* The NIV offers the translation: "one suitable for him." The connotation in Hebrew is the same as face-to-face, not side by side.

7. Is there an inference to a lack of intelligence or discernment in Eve's deception?

The word "deceive" means to thoroughly convince one to believe a lie. It means to supplant the truth with a lie. Eve's deception was attributed to the "subtlety" of the serpent and not to the lack of intelligence on her part.

. 2

3

SARAH'S STORY

Scriptural Reference: Genesis 12-18, 20-21

I. **The story of Abraham and Sarah depicts a prophetic journey.**
   It is an Old Testament story with New Testament implications:

*What shall we say then that Abraham our father, as pertaining to the flesh,
hath found? For if Abraham were justified by works, he hath whereof to
glory; but not before God. For what saith the scripture? Abraham believed
God, and it was counted unto him for righteousness...for the promise, that
he should be the heir of the world, was not to Abraham, or to his seed,
through the law, but through the righteousness of faith. Therefore it is of
faith, that it might be by grace; to the end the promise might be sure to all
the seed; not to that only which is of the law, but to that also which is of
faith of Abraham; who is the father of us all, (As it is written, I have made
thee a father of many nations,) before him whom he believed, even God,
who quickeneth the dead, and calleth those things which be not as though
they were. Who against hope believed in hope, that he might become the
father of many nations, according to that which was spoken, so shall thy
seed be. And being not weak in faith, he considered not his own body now
dead, when he was about an hundred years old, neither yet the deadness of
Sarah's womb: He staggered not at the promise of God through unbelief;
but was strong in faith, giving glory to God; and being fully persuaded
that, what he had promised, He was able also to perform. And therefore it
was imputed to him for righteousness. Now it was not written for his sake
alone, that it was imputed to him; but for us also, to whom it shall be imputed,
if we believe on him that raised up Jesus our Lord from the dead; Who was*

---

delivered for our offences, and was raised again for our justification.
(Romans 4:1-3,14,16-25)

Not as though the word of God hath taken none effect. For they are not all
Israel, which are of Israel: neither, because they are the seed of Abraham,
are they all children: but, in Isaac shall thy seed be called. That is, they
which are the children of the flesh, these are not the children of God: but the
children of the promise are counted for the seed. For this is the word of
promise, At this time I will come, and Sarah shall have a son. (Romans
9:6-9)

Even as Abraham believed God, and it was accounted to him for
righteousness. Know ye therefore that they which are of faith, the same are
the children of Abraham. And the scripture, foreseeing that God would
justify the heathen through faith, preached before the gospel unto Abraham,
saying, in thee shall all nations be blessed. So they which be of faith are
blessed with faithful Abraham......That the blessing of Abraham might come
on the Gentiles through Jesus Christ; that we might receive the promise of
the Spirit through faith...Now to Abraham and his seed were the promises
made. He saith not, and to seeds, as of many; but as of one, and to thy seed,
which is Christ.....For ye are all the children of God by faith in Christ Jesus.
For as many of you as have been baptized into Christ have put on Christ.
There is neither Jew nor Greek, there is neither bond nor free, there is neither
male nor female; for ye are all one in Christ. And if ye be Christ's, then are
ye Abraham's seed, and heirs according to the promise. (Galatians 3:6-
9,14, 16,26-29)

The redemptive significance of the story of Abraham is foundational to
Christianity. However, there is another part of this "history." There is
the record of Sarah which can be called "her-story."

The Scriptures have something significant to say about the wife of the
patriarch Abraham:

By faith Abraham, when he was called to go out into a place which he
should after receive for an inheritance, obeyed; and he went out, not knowing

whither he went. By faith he sojourned in the land of promise, as in a strange country, dwelling in tabernacles with Isaac and Jacob the heirs with him of the same promise; for he looked for a city which hath foundations, whose builder and maker is God. **Through faith also Sarai herself received strength to conceive seed, and was delivered of a child when she was past age, because she judged him faithful who had promised.** *(Hebrews 11:8-11)*

Sarah's story, though not separate from that of Abraham, has considerable significance. For the Scriptures clearly declare that **Sarah herself also received strength to conceive seed**. We shall examine the contribution of Sarah to this redemptive saga.

II. Genesis 12:1 records the original mandate to Abram to begin the journey.

   A. Sarai, Abram's wife, under the law of her culture was not obligated to go with him. The cultural laws stated that a woman should remain close to her "natural protectors" who would be her family. God had caused Sarai to wander with Abram, and it is believed that she had faith in a God that she did not know.

   B. The faithfulness of God is seen in the deliverance of Abram and Sarai in Egypt (Genesis 12:9-20). Because of famine, they go into Egypt and Abram entreats Sarai to pretend that she is his sister: *Please say you are my sister, that it may be well with me for your sake and that I may live because of you.* And indeed, Abram did live and was blessed because of Sarai. Pharaoh treated Abram well for Sarai's sake. And God delivered Sarai from the house of Pharaoh.

III. In Genesis 13, God promises to bless Abram and make of him a great nation. In Genesis 15:1-4, God declares that Eliezer will not be Abraham's heir, but *a son coming from your own body will be your heir...* **In Genesis 16 there is no specific reference to Sarai's knowledge of the promise. Therefore, it may be a speculative**

conclusion that the offer of her maidservant to Abraham indicates some awareness.

A. Sarai was not attempting to help God. In that culture, if a woman was barren, her husband could cast her out. Sarai was well within the norms of tradition and culture to request Abram to raise up seed from the maid. It is also apparent that Sarai is aware of the promise made Abram.

B. The norm of culture and tradition is further demonstrated in Abraham's response to the knowledge that he and Sarah would have a son between them; for in Genesis 17:15-17 it is recorded that Abraham laughed at the promise that two very old people would have a child. It appears that Abraham had accepted that God would fulfill His promise, but Abraham was amazed at the method: *Then Abraham fell upon his face, and laughed, and said in his heart, shall a child be born unto him that is an hundred years old? And shall Sarah, that is ninety years old, bear?*

C. In Genesis 18:10-15, the norm of culture and tradition is further demonstrated. Sarai, like Abraham, may have believed the promise of a seed and sent Abraham unto Hagar. But Sarai laughs when she overhears the promise that she will be part of the method of this fulfillment: *Therefore, Sarah laughed within herself saying, after I am waxed old shall I have pleasure, my lord being old also?* Sarai's laughter was perhaps over the promise of her bearing a son. In V.13, the Divine inquiry about the laughter of Sarai is suggested to be a rebuke to Abraham. For Abraham had previously been informed that the seed would come naturally through Sarai and himself (Genesis 17:14-19) but apparently he had failed to notify Sarai of this dimension of the promise. So the Lord eradicates their doubt with the question: *Is anything too hard for the Lord?*

D. Genesis 17:15-16 records the Divine mandate to change the name of Sarai to Sarah. The reason given is simple: *And I will bless her, and give thee a son also of her; yea I will bless her, and she shall be a mother of nations; kings of people shall be of her.* The name Sarah means *prince, chief, and commander.* This represents a change in the status of Sarah. She is now a matriarch, a woman of authority and power. The prophetic promise is that nations and kings of people shall come from her.

E. These series of events were vital to demonstrate the role of Abraham and Sarah as co-participators and co-laborers with God in bringing forth the promised seed, Isaac. It further demonstrates that the Sarah/Hagar episode was a norm of culture and tradition and not an effort to supercede God. In fact, because Sarah requested Abraham to cast Hagar and Ishmael out of the compound, Hagar received her freedom and both of them received a covenant promise of God. (Genesis 21:9-21).

DISCUSSION

1. How has the Sarah/Hagar episode been used to indict Sarah?

2. What significance was attached to the changing of the name "Sarai" to "Sarah?"

3. How was the faithfulness of God demonstrated in the deliverance of Abram and Sarai in Egypt?

4. What events demonstrated the role of Abraham and Sarah as co-participators in bringing forth the promised seed, Isaac?

5. How was God's faithfulness demonstrated to Hagar and Ishmael after their dismissal?

.
.
.
.
. 3

4

OLD TESTAMENT WOMEN'S ROLES

The roles played by men in God's redemptive plan are evident throughout the Old Testament. However, a careful examination will reveal significant contributions by women. Their roles ranged from prophets, musicians, judges, counselors, deliverers, to founders of cities. In this section, we will examine some of the co-laborship roles played by men and women while also exploring some of the unfamiliar accomplishments of women.

➤ The first female that God spoke to was Eve. Genesis 3:13

➤ God spoke to Hagar giving her a promise. Genesis 16:8-11

➤ God spoke to Rebekah regarding the children in her womb. Genesis 25:22

➤ Women were used in the making of the tabernacle of the Lord. Exodus 38:8

➤ Women took the vow of the Nazarite. Numbers 6:1-27

➤ Rahab was a harlot used by God. She aided Israel in the victory over the Philistines when she hid the spies in her home. Her name means freedom from narrowness. She is the mother of Boaz, the grandfather of David, progenitor of Jesus. Joshua 2

➤ Jael was a secret ally of Israel who offered Sisera, an enemy of Israel, sanctuary in her tent. While he slept she drove a tent peg into his head and killed him, thus fulfilling Deborah's prophetic word to Barak, saying a woman would steal his glory. Judges 4:17-22

➤ God spoke to Samson's mother regarding his birth and call. Judges 13

➤ Naomi and Ruth were two widows functioning in a hostile world who showed both strength and character and integrity. Ruth is the grandmother of David.

➤ Abigail saved David and her household by preventing David from committing massacre on the household of Nabal. She is considered a wise woman because of her act of intercession and intervention. I Samuel 25

➤ A wise woman of Tekoa was sent to intercede for Absalom. II Samuel 14:2

➤ Sherrah, daughter of Ephraim, built cities. (II Chronicles 7:24) Her name means kinswoman. She founded two cities, Beth-Horons "upper and lower," and Uzzen-Sherrah. I Chronicles 7:24

➤ Heman, the king's seer, had fourteen sons and three daughters who assisted their father in providing music in the house of the Lord. I Chronicles 25:5-6

➤ Women were involved with the restoration of the wall after the Babylonian captivity. Nehemiah 3:12

➤ Esther was a very young woman hidden by God to bring deliverance to her nation. As queen of Persia she responded to the reality of her birth and the desire of God's heart to preserve the remnant of Israel.

➢ Job gave an inheritance to his daughters as well as his sons. Job 42:15

➢ Women were evangelists. *The Lord gave the word; great was the company of those who published it.* ("Tsaba, here translated as "company" means "a female mass of people.") Psalms 68:11

➢ God spoke to Mary about the birth of Jesus. Luke 1:28

WOMEN PROPHETS

The office of the prophet was one of the highest offices in the Old Testament and women prophets were equally as valuable as their male counterparts.

➢ **Miriam** - *Then Miriam, sister of Aaron, took timbrels in her hand; and all the women went out after her with timbrels and with dances. Exodus 15:20 (NKJ)*

As Miriam was one of the leaders of the nation along with her brothers, Aaron and Moses. (Micah 6:4)

➢ **Deborah** - *Now Deborah, a prophetess, the wife of Lapidoth, was judging Israel at that time. Judges 4:4 (NKJ) And she would sit under the palm tree of Deborah between Ramah and Bethel in the mountains of Ephraim. And the children of Israel came up to her for Judgment. Judges 4:5 (NKJ)*

She was a military leader and considered a mother in Israel. Her name means "bee."

➢ **Huldah -** *So Hilkiah the priest, Ahikam, Achbor, Shaphan, and Asaiah went to Huldah the prophetess, the wife of Shallum the son of Tikvah,* *the son of Harhas, keeper of the wardrobe.* (She dwelt in Jerusalem in the second quarter.) *And they spoke with her. II Kings 22:14* (NKJ)

> **Isaiah's Wife** - She authenticated the newly found book of the law for them. Through her prophetic decree she gave judgment and direction to Israel, bringing them to repentance and worship of Jehovah. Isaiah 8:3

> Noadiah - *...Remember Tobiah and Sanballat, oh my God, because of what they have done; remember also the prophetess, Noadiah, and the rest of the prophets who have been trying to intimidate me. Nehemiah 6:14 (KJV)*

> Noadiah means 1) Jehovah convenes, and 2) one who makes men afraid.

OLD TESTAMENT COUPLES

> Abraham and Sarah
> Genesis 12 - 18
> *... Abraham obeyed Sarah ...*

> Elhannah/Hannah
> I Samuel 1:10-18
> *... Hannah prayed and travailed for the child ...*

> Rebecca and Isaac
> Genesis 24
> ... Isaac, the promised seed, and Rebecca brought forth the patriarch, Israel (prince of God) ...

> Manoah and his wife
> Judges 13
> ... Manoah feared that he and his wife would die because they had "seen God". His wife quieted his fears assuring him of God's

pleasure by his acceptance of their sacrifice...
... both parents protected their son's (Samson) choice of a
wife ...

➢ Hosea and Gomer
Hosea
... God used this couple as a metaphor to show His love,
faithfulness, and longsuffering ...

PROPHECIES TO WOMEN
Anointed by the Holy Spirit

1. *Rise up, you women who are at ease, hear my voice; you complacent daughters, give ear to my speech. Isaiah 32:9 (NKJ)*

2. In a year and (some) days you will be troubled, you complacent women; for the vintage will fail, the gathering will not come. Isaiah 32:10 (NKJ)

3. *....until the Spirit is poured upon us from on high, and the wilderness becomes a fruitful field, and the fruitful field is counted as a forest.* Isaiah 32:15 (NKJ)

4. *And it shall come to pass afterward that I will pour out My Spirit on all flesh; your sons and your daughters shall prophesy, your old men shall dream dreams, your young men shall see visions;...* Joel 2:28 (NKJ)

5. *And also on (My) menservants and on (My) maidservants I will pour out My Spirit in those days.* Joel 2:29 (NKJ)

6. *But this is what was spoken by the prophet Joel...* Acts 2:16 (NKJ) *...'and it shall come to pass in the last days, says God, that I will pour out of My Spirit on all flesh; your sons and your daughters shall prophesy, your young men shall see visions, your old men shall dream dreams'...* Acts 2:17 (NKJ)

7. *... and on My menservants and on My maidservants I will pour out My Spirit in those days; and they shall prophesy.* Acts 2:18 (NKJ)

8. *... The Lord gave the word; great (was) the company of those who proclaimed (it) ...* Psalms 68:11 (NKJ)

DISCUSSION

1. What are some of the implications of the prophecy of Joel 2:28 and the fulfillment recorded in Acts 2:16-17 regarding men and women?

2. What is the implication of the story of Manoah and his wife on the order of revelation?

3. What other examples demonstrate a woman as the primary recipient of revelation?

4. List as many different categories in which women served in the Old Testament.

5. Discuss some of the lessons gathered from the roles played by Deborah, Miriam, and Huldah.

6. If it is a sign of the new age for both men and women to prophesy, discuss some of the reasons given for prohibiting women from preaching in the Church.

5

NEW TESTAMENT WOMEN

Jesus brought about a full emancipation to womanhood through his teachings and his attitude toward women. In this section we shall explore the emerging change in the status of women as a direct result of the public ministry of Jesus. Women played significant roles during the life and times of the Lord Jesus as the Gospels will reveal to us. Their roles in the New Testament Church will be seen as we journey through the epistles.

Jesus' Behavior Towards Women

> ➢ Jesus touched "unclean" women. Matthew 9:20-22

> ➢ The resurrected Christ was first seen by women. Matthew 28:1-10

> ➢ Jesus allowed women to touch him. Mark 5:34

> ➢ Jesus ate with harlots and sinners. Luke 7:36-50

> ➢ Jesus allowed women to minister to him. Luke 8:1-3

➤ Jesus taught women. Luke 10:38-42 (Rabbis refused.)

➤ Jesus prompted women to evangelize.
John 4:28-29, 39, 42

WOMEN WHO MINISTERED TO JESUS

➤ Mary, the mother of James and John; and the mother of Zebedee's children

➤ Mary of Magdala

➤ JoAnna, wife of Herod Antipas

➤ Susanna

➤ Mary, the Lord's mother

➤ Mary, the wife of Cleophas

NEW TESTAMENT PRESENCE OF WOMEN

➤ Luke 1-2 - Elizabeth, the mother of John

➤ Matthew 1 - Mary, the mother of Jesus

➤ Mark 5:34 - Jesus heals a woman

➤ Luke 10:38-40 - Jesus taught women and men

➤ Luke 8:1-3 - Many women ministered to Jesus: Mary Magdalene, Johanna, the wife of Chuza

➤ Luke 7:12-15 - Jesus heals the son of a widow

- Acts 1:14 - Women were in the upper room at the outpouring of the Holy Spirit

- Acts 5:14 - Women were among the first Christian converts

- Acts 9:1-2 - Women were among those persecuted by Saul

- Acts 9:36 - A certain disciple named Dorcas

- Acts 16:13 - Paul preached to the women at Philippi

- Acts 13:50 - Women resisted Paul at Antioch, in Asia Minor

- Romans 16:1 - Paul calls Phoebe "prostatis" or "presiding officer"

- Romans 16:7 - Junia noted among the apostles

WOMEN IN NEW TESTAMENT MINISTRY

- **Priscilla**
  *Greet Priscilla and Aquila, my fellow workers in Christ Jesus...
  Romans 16:3* (Priscilla's name actually appears first in the
  Greek: possibly indicating that she was the primary
  instructor.)

  *Now a certain Jew named Appolos, born at Alexandria, an eloquent
  man (and) mighty in the Scriptures, came to Ephesus. This man
  had been instructed in the way of the Lord; and being fervent in
  spirit, he spoke and taught accurately the things of the Lord, though
  he knew only the baptism of John. So he began to speak boldly in
  the synagogue. When Aquilla and Priscilla heard him, they took
  him aside and explained to him the way of God more accurately.
  Acts 18:24-26* (Husband and wife pastors and teachers.)

➢ **Phoebe**
I commend to you Phoebe our sister, who is a servant of the church in Cenchrea Romans (Servant ("diakonas" - minister) is translated 20 times as minister and this word is used in its masculine form here. It also means, "one having areas of authority.")

...that you may receive her in whatever business she has need of you; for indeed she has been a helper of many and of myself also..."
Romans 16:2

➢ **Tryphena and Tryphosa**
Greet Tryphena and Tryphosa, who have labored in the Lord. Greet the beloved Persis, who labored much in the Lord. Romans 16:12

➢ **Euodias and Syntyche**
I implore Euodia and I implore Syntyche to be of the same mind in the Lord. Philippians 4:3

➢ **Junia, an apostle**
Greet Andronicus and Junia, my kinsmen and my fellow prisoners, who are of note among the apostles, who also were in Christ before me. Romans 16:7

➢ **Anna the Prophetess**
Now there was one, Anna, a prophetess, the daughter of Phanuel, of the tribe of Asher. She was of a great age, and had lived with a husband seven years from her virginity.... Luke 2:36

➢ **Women served as teachers. II John 1:1, Philippians 4:2-3**

➢ **Women served as evangelists. John 4**

➢ **Women served as deacons. I Timothy 3:8-11**

➢ **Women served as prophets, Phillip's four daughters. Acts 21:9**

➤ **Women headed house churches:**
  ◆ Chloe - I Corinthians 1:11
  ◆ Nemphia - Collossians 4:15
  ◆ Mary, the mother of John Mark - Acts 12:12
  ◆ Lydia - Acts 16:15
  ◆ Apphia - Philemon 1:2

DISCUSSION

1. Compare the roles played by women in the New Testament and the Old Testament.

2. List additional teachings of Jesus that influenced the relationship between men and women.

3. Discuss the implications of the teaching of Jesus recorded in Matthew 19:3-9 on divorce and the rights of women. How much had traditions differed from God's original intentions regarding the issue of marriage?

4. What conclusions can be drawn from the Gospels and the epistles regarding the new status of women?

.
.
.
.
. 5

6

HEAD/HEADSHIP

What is the concept of head/headship as it relates to the home and the church? Paul makes mention of the term in Ephesians 5:23 and I Corinthians 11:3. Does the term imply ruler, dictator, or Lord? In this section we will explore terminology and ancient culture and custom in an effort to fully understand the concept of head/headship.

The issue of head covering (I Corinthians 11:8-10) was born out of culture and custom.[1] Culturally, respectable women covered their heads. A Jewish custom held that a woman, when praying was to honor the authority of her husband by having her head covered (I Corinthians 11:5). Head covering in public also separated "respectable" women from harlots and pagans. Ancient superstition held that evil spirits would seduce or attack a woman whose head was uncovered publicly.

The Hebrew word for "head" is *rosh*, meaning, "first in order" and can also be translated as "first, beginning, captain, chief and ruler."[2] It is used as ruler only twice in the Old Testament. (Isaiah 29:10 and Deuteronomy 1:13)

The New Testament word for head is *kephale*, which has two meanings. One meaning is *chief*. Speaking of Jesus Christ as the Head of the Church. Colossians 1:15-18 says, *He is the image of the invisible God, the firstborn over all creation. For by him all things were created; things in heaven and on earth, visible and invisible, whether thrones or powers or rulers or authorities;*

---

all things were created by him and for him. He is before all things, and in him all things hold together. And he is the head of the body, the church; he is the beginning and the firstborn from among the dead, so that in everything he might have the supremacy. Kephale also means *the first one into battle;* it is a military term. It further means the leader by example, not command. It has over 25 possible figurative meanings in addition to the literal meaning, **none of which** are "authority, superior, rank, or director."[3]

Another Greek word for head is *arche,* which means leader and point of origin. We get such words as "archtype," "archives," and archeology from this source.[4] Forms of *arche* are used throughout the New Testament in Paul's writings, to designate the head or leader of a group of people such as magistrate, chief, prince, ruler, and head.[5]

Paul more often used the word *Kephale* when referring to the head. In English the word "head" literally means physical head of one's body. In Colossians 2:19, Paul describes Christ as, *the head, from whom all the body, nourished and knit together by joints and ligaments, grows with increase, which is from God.* This passage refers to Christ's government. It represents Him as the supporter, nourisher, and builder of the body, its Savior.

We get the words regarding headship first in Genesis 3:16, and another reference in Ephesians 5:23. No other word can be found throughout the Old Testament that seems to support the interpretation that men are to govern (rule) their wives.

Liefield and Tucker point out, in the book, <u>Daughters of the Church</u>, that in Ephesians 5:23-29, the mention of head is immediately followed by a reference to Christ as "savior of the body."[6] Some authorities feel that Christ is the example for husbands by bringing wholeness and completeness to His bride, the Church. The passage goes on to speak of Christ loving the Church, giving Himself up for her, making her holy, cleansing her and making her radiant, feeding and caring for her. It should be noted that Paul never mentioned "leadership" or "authority" in reference to marriage, and the husband is never portrayed as "ruler" in relation to the wife submitting to the husband.

Ancient marriage customs differed much from our western concepts.[7] Before the wedding day the "bride-bath" took place in a designated place. On the morning of the wedding, the bride was ceremoniously washed, clothed, and draped with the bridal wreath and veil. She was presented to the groom spiritually clean from washing in sacred springs and physically clean from washing on the wedding day. She was without spot or blemish, pure and holy, according to custom. Paul used this custom to illustrate the relationship of Christ and the Church (Ephesians 5:25-27). There were several types of marriages in the Hebrew culture:

In the "Beena" type of marriage the husband severed relations with his own family and united with the family of his wife. The offspring of this type of marriage took the mother's name, and the genealogy was reckoned in her line. Biblical examples of this are found in Ezra 2:61 and Nehemiah 7:63.

The "Ishi" marriage was the most common form among the Hebrews. It was the customary union of a free man and a free woman. The wife received from her husband a dowry and a pledge of support and maintenance that was in accordance with the custom of Jewish husbands who worked for their wives, held them in honor, and supported and maintained them.

"Baal," another type of marriage, signifies master, possessor, or owner. If a father were in poverty, he could sell his daughter to an Israelite with a view to marriage. He could never sell her to a foreigner. If the marriage was not consummated, the husband must allow for her to be redeemed. This type of marital union was of a master/bondmaiden. If the husband contracted for a second wife, he was obligated to continue maintaining the "Baal" wife. If he did not do so, she was allowed to go free, and he was to divorce her.

The last type of marriage was the "Leverate" type. This was the union of a man with the childless widow of a deceased brother. The firstborn seed of this marriage took the name of the deceased brother, and inherited the estate of this deceased brother. This custom was handed down from the patriarchal age. (Genesis 38:8), and it's purpose was to preserve the family's name and inheritance. (Deuteronomy 25:6,9).[8]

Genesis 2:24, "*Therefore, a man shall leave his father and mother and be joined to his wife, and they shall be one flesh.*" God's laws were designed to protect women from wicked men by allowing for the man to reside with the wife's family during the first year of marriage. God did not make the wife superior to the husband, nor did He make her subordinate to her husband.

Judges 15 saw Samson visiting his Philistine wife, for she remained with her people. The offspring in such a marriage belonged to the woman's family, not the man's.

When God separated Abraham and Sarah from their idolatrous relatives, (Genesis 12:4), He virtually ordained Sarah, after matriarchal custom, the ruling head of the tribe.

Sarah, a primary Biblical personality in the Old Testament, was a female chief, and her name, which means *Chieftainess*, supports this. Sar is the regular old term for *Chief*. Sarah lived independently of Abraham at Mamre while Abraham lived at Beersheba; it is said that Abraham came to mourn for her and bury her. Sarah's position, during her wanderings with Abraham and in her later life, was not that of a secluded dependency, but rather that of an independent head of the tribe, and tribal mother.

Historically women have been taught that man is the ruling head over them, whether in marriage, church, or business. Contrary to this teaching, we see that Paul was not talking about headship by "lording," but by example. One who is the true head does not rule by spouting out orders and demands, but is one who directs by example. More on "head" is covered in Chapter 8.

DISCUSSION

1. Discuss your concept of head/headship and compare with the material contained in this chapter.

2. Explore the differences between a marriage where the husband and wife experience an equal relationship with the "Baal" type marriage.

3. Discuss the benefits and disadvantages of a marriage based on "equal partnership" between the husband and wife.

4. Discuss the benefits and disadvantages of a marriage based on the "subordination" of the wife to the husband.

5. List five ways that the concept of head/headship contained in this section could influence the attitudes and roles of men and women in the marketplace.

Chapter Six Endnotes

[1] George M. Lamsa, *New Testament Commentary* (Philadelphia: A. J. Holman, 1945), pp 271-272.

[2] John Temple Bristow, *What Paul Really Said About Women* (San Francisco: Harper & Row, 1988), pp 35-36.

[3] Gretchen Baebelein Hull, *Equal To Serve* (Grand Rapids: Baker Books, 1991), p 193. Hull observes evidence from the ancient literature that *kephale* is used as "source" as well as "authority over."

[4] Bristow, 36.

[5] Susan C. Hyatt, *In The Spirit We're Equal: The Spirit, The Bible, and Women, A Revival Perspective* (Dallas: Hyatt Press, 1998), pp 248-255.

[6] Liefield and Tucker, *Daughters of the Church: Women and Ministry From New Testament Times to the Present* (Grand Rapids: Zondervan 1986); pp 454-455.

[7] Bishop K. C. Pillai, *Light Through An Eastern Window* (New York: Robert Speller & Sons, 1963), pp 1-23.

[8] Lee Anna Starr, *The Bible Status of Woman* (Zarephath, N.J.: Pillar of Fire, 1955), pp 94-99.

7

COVERING

Etymology is the study of the roots or primitive forms from which words are derived. Etymology should never be considered apart from usage or context. For example, the English word "nice" comes from the Latin *nescius*, "ignorant." Obviously, there is no connection between the current meaning of "nice" and it etymology. Let us consider the word "cover" which has been used to express a social and juridical relation of the man over the woman. The word "cover" or "covering" is derived from kalypto (to cover, hide), **kalymma** (covering, veil). The basic meaning seems to be "to bury" or "to hide." The cloud covers the tent in Exodus 24:15-16 and the priests cover themselves when ministering. A figurative use for the covering of sin appears in Psalms 32:5. In the New Testament, we find James 5:20 and I Peter 4:8 are based on Proverbs 10:12 when they speak about the covering of sin by loving action.

The word is also linked to "veil" or "head covering." In the Old Testament Moses wears a "cover" over his face in Exodus 34:33 to either protect the people from the divine glory or to protect the divine glory from the profanity of the people. In the New Testament the term occurs in I Corinthians 11:6-7. Paul addresses the cultural significance of headwear and also the significance in the Christian church. The Corinthians were making an issue of those women who were coming into the temple with their heads uncovered. Paul was simply trying to take the emphasis off of people looking at the outward appearance of those who prayed or prophesied to decide whether they were spiritual or not. He admonished them in v:11-16, *In the Lord, however, woman is not independent of man nor is man independent of woman for as woman came from man, so also man was born of woman. But everything comes from God. Judge for yourselves: is it proper for a woman to pray to God with her head uncovered? Does not the very nature of things teach you that if a man has long hair, it is a disgrace to him, but that if a woman has long hair, it is her glory? For long hair is given to her as a covering. If anyone wants to be contentious about this, we have no other practice, nor do the churches of God.*

The word "cover" or "covering" has taken on a governmental significance. In the New Testament, I Corinthians 11:3-16 is often used to imply that the woman should be "covered" or "superintended" or "administered" by the man. This conclusion is seemingly based upon the chronology of the formation of Adam and Eve, the nature of Eve's transgression (the woman was deceived), and the inference that women are "weaker vessels." Eve is alleged to have departed from the "covering" of Adam and conversed with the serpent and, thereby initiated the transgression. From a practical standpoint, the woman is not to make decisions nor initiate judgments without the consent and counsel of the man. The man becomes the "covering" for the woman and ultimately for the family.

The concept has raised much controversy in religious circles. The governmental implication seems to subordinate the female to the male and establishes an order of revelation that begins with the Holy Ghost and is related to the man and ultimately to the woman and the family. Any woman that is in ministry or in an occupation that does not have governmental relationship with a man is a woman in error according to the concept. If a woman initiates a business, organization, ministry, or a relationship with the awareness of a male "covering," then she is operating according to proper spiritual protocol according to this model.

Let us examine the origin of the concept. The first reference to the concept of "covering" is found in Genesis 3:7, 21 when they concealed their nakedness with fig leaves. The occasion for this act of "covering" by God was the transgression of the man and the woman. Hence, the first appearance of the concept of "covering" is in its relationship with sin. The prophet Jeremiah echoes this meaning of the term when he cries, *We lie down in our shame, and our confusion covereth us; for we have sinned against the Lord our God, we and our fathers, from our youth even unto this day, and have not obeyed the voice of the Lord our God.* (3:25).

Another Old Testament reference is to found in Ruth 3:1-13 in which Ruth is instructed by Naomi to lie at the feet of kinsman Boaz after he has eaten and is drunk. If Boaz accepts Ruth, he will spread his garment over her according to the text: *"And he said, who art thou? And she answered, I am Ruth thine handmaid, spread therefore thy skirt over thine handmaid; for thou art a near kinsman."* The cultural context is very significant here. According to Mosaic law, when a brother died having no child, his wife was not to marry a stranger, but must marry her husband's brother in order that he might raise offspring through his brother (Deuteronomy 25:5). This law was enacted by Moses in order to keep the land in the family (Ruth 4:1-6). The maidens of one tribe whose father had no male heir and who had inherited his land were not to marry among other tribes, in order that the land might not change hands from one tribe to another[1] (Numbers 27:8-11). The expression "spread thy skirt" imports protection, and here signifies protection of a conjugal character. When marriages are solemnized among the Jews, the man throws the skirt or his robe over his wife and covers her head with it[2]. The social and cultural context of this event must be noted since these ordinances are no longer continued.

Another New Testament reference is to be found in James 5:19-20: *Brethern, if anyone among you wanders from the truth, and someone turns him back, let him know that he who turns a sinner from the error of his ways will save a soul from death and cover a multitude of sin.* Here, as in I Peter 4:8, the reference is based on Proverbs 10:12 when they speak of covering of sin by loving action. Love insures access to divine forgiveness. The concept of "covering" here is more redemptive for the acts of reproof, and correction turns the individual back to the truth. The relationship between the two individuals involved here is not governmental but relational. There is no sense of subordination nor any reference to a hierarchical relationship between the "restorer" and the one "being restored."

The contemporary concept of "covering," in which there is an inference to a governmental relationship between husband and wife or between men and women finds no parallel in either the New Testament nor the Old Testament. In fact, the Scriptures constantly speak of a mutual and a collaborative relationship that ought to exist between the husband and wife. Covenant partnership is both contractual and governmental since it provides for mutual counsel and consent on the part of the man and the woman. This is clearly stated in I Corinthians 7:3-4 in which the conjugal relationship between a husband and wife is a collateral agreement.

When the term "covering" is used in reference to the restoration of a fallen individual, there is a sense of beauty and love. A weakened member is disabled by a transgression. A spiritual helper comes along and provides help by creating an atmosphere of confidentiality, patience, and love while providing the necessary ingredients required for restoration. To "cover" does not mean, in these instances, to erase or to deny the reality of the transgression. It is the provision of a "bandage" of security, confidentiality and truth necessary for healing to occur without the intrusion of antagonistic ingredients such as outside criticism, harsh judgments, or retributive justice. This is a beautiful concept of "covering" since it implies creating an atmosphere of restoration and recovery. Obviously, this same concept can occur in a marriage in which the husband or the wife provides the same atmosphere of love, nurturing, and confidentiality.

In conclusion, the concept of "covering" has many spiritual, social, and governmental implications. However, it is not a gender specific concept. It is an act of love, benevolence, healing, and restoration; and the governmental implication is to be found in the statement: *Ye that are spiritual, cover.*

DISCUSSION

1. Discuss your concept of "covering" and the ways in which it agrees or disagrees with the material in this section.

2. How does the concept of "covering" relate to the process of the restoration of an estranged member of the Church?

3. Can a woman be the head of an organization or a business with out male oversight?

4. Discuss ways in which a husband and a wife can "cover" one another.

Chapter Seven Endnotes

[1] George M. Lamsa, *Old Testament Light* (Philadelphia: A. J. Holman, 1945) pp. 308.

[2] James M. Freeman, *Manners and Customs of the Bible* (Plainfield: Logos International, 1972) pp.129.

SUBMISSION

Submission is a term that has been greatly misunderstood within the church world. The term has often been associated with the doctrine of authoritative male headship and female subordination. In this section we shall explore the origin of the term and its harmony with biblical teaching.

The English word "submit" finds its orgin in the Greek word *hupotasso* in the New Testament. Briefly, *hupotasso* has several meanings: (1) to show responsible behavior toward others (I Cor. 14:32,35; Rom. 13:1; I Pet. 2:13), (2) to be brought into a sphere of influence, and (3) to add or unite one person or thing with another (Eph. 5:22-23,33). The term in its original context does not infer the unilateral obedience and subjugation of one person to another. There is more of an idea of mutuality and interdependence rather than patriarchy/matriarchy and authority over/subordination to others.[1]

According to Dr. Katherine Bushnell, the noun "subjection" is not found in classical Greek, outside of the New Testament.[2] This term was coined to describe relationships peculiar to believers. Upon careful analysis, the word describes the Christian grace of voluntarily yielding one's preference to another rather than the assertion of one's individual rights. Schleusner's Greek-Latin Lexicon to the Septuagint declares that this verb does not always "carry the thought of servile subjection."[3] Luke records the story of Jesus at the age of 12 being separated from his parents briefly. When they discovered him in the temple, he returned with them to Nazareth and was "subject to them" once again. Catherine Kroeger claims that this account did not imply obedience but rather the reentering of Jesus into the sphere of his parents and his identification and integration with them in their world of everyday life.[4]

To limit the concept of submission to subjection and to omit its contextual meaning creates confusion. The words "subjection" and "obedience" do not carry the same scope of meaning in the original Greek. The word "subjection" is taken from *hupo* and carries the meaning of being "next after" or "under," and *tasso*, means "to arrange after" or "to arrange under." In a business relationship between two people, each of them must arrange or harmonize their views and preferences for the common good of the business. Each of the partners must yield their opinions to the other. They will not resolve a conflict of opinion if one assumes the right to command the other. Gundry calls this equalizing principle as a sort of voluntary raising everyone else to your own personal level of importance and worthiness.[5] John Bristow cites the German translation of the word, *sich unterstellen*, to mean the placing of yourself at the disposition of another.[6] In a military context, the term can refer to the equal sharing of tasks, to support, to fulfill ones part of the assignment.

Let us go deeper to the root of the controversy surrounding this term. In our society, churches, and homes, we have been exposed to several types of submission: cultural, traditional, and contemporary. Basically, we have been taught that each of these focuses on one message, i.e. "women are to submit always and without qualification." However, the Bible says that women are to submit "in the Lord," which brings about a new dynamic of relationship. Women are now free to judge what is "in the Lord." However, if we are to be well studied, we must also examine the fact that the Bible also teaches that we are to *submit to one another* (Ephesians 5:21). Submission, then, is volitional, and the sole purpose is to reflect Christ Jesus. It is without respect to age, gender, sex, nationality, and economic status. This submission is Biblical Submission because it reflects the character of God. It is totally inclusive. And this is where we are ultimately called to live; <u>inclusively and beyond gender.</u>

Now, let's directly address Paul and Peter. When they were using the word "submit," they were giving Christians a way of coping within a culture hostile to the teachings of Jesus.   Paul writes,   . . .*subjecting yourself one to another in the fear of Christ* (Ephesians 5:21). Peter likewise addresses the same societal situations writing, *Yea all of you be subject to another, and be clothed with humility* (I Peter 5:5). Being subject to or subjecting oneself to another deals with mutual respect one for the other, and it should not convey the loss of one's right to make choices. It should not be taught as an attitude or action required only for women in relation to husbands or any male figure.

Peter's theme for writing his first letter centers around Christian life and duty. Christians at that time were a minority. Peter encourages them to realize that they are to be a demonstration to the world, and that the power of God within enables them to live in a hostile world. In I Peter 2:13, Peter writes, *Submit yourselves for the Lord's sake to every human institution . . . , for such is the will of God that by doing right you may silence the ignorance of foolish men.* Peter further tells servants to submit to their master whether good or evil as witness proving who the greater master is. He tells them that they are not bound by the values of the world, but they have a higher value because they believe in and are under the Lordship of Christ Jesus. Therefore, the people observing them should see an evident difference. Followers of Christ show 1) obedience to and 2) respect for authority. They should not use their spiritual freedom for an occasion to sin; rather, they are to live as servants of God. I Peter 2:11. *Conduct yourselves honorably among the Gentiles, so that, though they malign you as evildoers, they may see your honorable deeds and glorify God. . . .* Peter continues to emphasize his point in verse 13 of chapter 2, *For the Lord's sake accept the authority of every human institution.;* and in verses 15 - 17, *For it is God's will that by doing right you shall silence the ignorance of the foolish. As servants of God, live as free people, yet do not use your freedom as a pretext for evil. Honor everyone. Love the family of believers. Fear God. Honor the Emperor.*

Next, Peter elucidates proper behavior of slaves who are believers towards their masters: Verse 18 - 20, *Slaves, accept the authority of your master with all defense, not only those who are kind and gentle but also, those who are harsh. For it is a credit to you if, being aware of God, you endure pain while suffering unjustly. . . but if you endure when you do right and suffer for it, you have God's approval. For to this you have been called, because Christ also suffered for you, leaving you an example, so that you should follow in his steps.*

Now, following the elucidation for slaves, in the same mind, Peter speaks to the women. The ultimate emphasis to the women in chapter three is for them to win their husbands to Christ. Women at that time were in a precarious position - the culture demanded subservient submission to the husband. However, when women became believers, they were not bound by the cultural traditions - they had a higher law - the law of God which gave them a new freedom and independence. Peter basically says to them, "if submitting to your husbands will win them to Christ, then do it." However, nowhere does the Bible suggest that they were to submit to abuse. These women joined to unbelievers, by their demonstration of love, forgiveness, character, prayer, and integrity, were to win their husbands to Christ. Peter urges them not to spend all of their time adorning their bodies, but the adorning of the inward man. He considers lasting beauty a *gentle and quiet spirit, which is precious in the sight of God.* Again, this did not mean that a woman should accept abuse in her gentleness and quietness. Nor should this statement lead one to assume that the women were in an uproar, loud and not gentle. Such assumptions provoke us to misinterpretation. Finally, Peter uses Sarah as an example. Sarah is recorded as referring to Abraham as "Lord." She used the word, "Lord" when she had been informed that she would bear a son, Isaac, from her own body. She did not use the word to convey subservience, but it is used in respect to her husband. Historians report that the term is actually one of endearment as in "honey" or "sir." It did not mean rulership. Keep in mind that scriptures also say that "Abraham obeyed Sarah", demonstrating or showing mutual respect and submission. Peter in 3:7 reinforces his point of mutual submission by informing the men that in the same way the women are to live, "..so are you." You show consideration to your wives in your life together, paying honor to the woman as the "weaker vessel, since they too are also heirs of the gracious gift of life - so that nothing may hinder your prayers." The term "weaker vessel" is a cultural term; women of that time were considered weaker in every aspect: physically, intellectually, and spiritually. Peter says that men were to pay honor to this person whom they have always considered weaker. But now, she is an heir, and if they fail to respect her, their prayers will be hindered.

History and science have shown that women are not morally or mentally weaker than men. Women more often than not were, indeed, physically weaker in Biblical days. However, in modern society, women have entered many areas of what has been termed a man's domain. Today, women body build, play professional tennis, basketball, golf, and many other physically demanding sports. Women have entered the business world, the scientific community, the law enforcement community, the medical community, and many other male dominated arenas. Thus, this statement of "weaker vessel" is a culturally specific one and not a judgement upon women's abilities to function in independent excellence.

Finally, as we re-read and re-study I Peter, we must understand that Peter, in this letter, is addressing the conduct of Christians: 1) conduct of all, 2) conduct of those who suffer for Christ, 3) conduct of Elders (I Peter 5:1-4), and 4) conduct of Young Men (I Peter 5:5-10).

When Paul used the term "submission" in reference to women, he was addressing specific situations. Paul was not giving blanket instructions for the behavior of all women in the Church Universal. I would also encourage you to study Colossians 3 with your focus on the context of "putting on the new man in Christ Jesus" and the cultural challenges that the early Christians faced.

This scripture passage of I Corinthians 11: 2-16 has been used to subjugate women and to imply that man is her "covering." Without knowledge of the Genesis story and the culture which Paul was addressing, one could conclude that misconception. However, to clear up any misconception let's review this scripture in light of its true meaning. Paul is addressing the traditions that he had given them in reference to the traditions and practices that they lived by. He is giving instruction in deportment during worship services. He begins, *Be imitators of me, just as I also am of Christ. Now I praise you because you remember me in everything and hold firmly to the traditions, just as I delivered them to you.* In verse 3, Paul begins to discuss their concerns, some of which require his establishment of the Source of all things, Christ. We must remember Paul is speaking to a Gentile congregation, which would be ignorant of much Jewish history. Thus, the fact that God is the source of all is primary to their understanding of their faith.

Paul wants to remind them of a Jewish tradition delivered to them wherein the term "head" is used, *But I want you to understand that Christ is the head of every man, and the husband is the head of his wife, and God is the head of Christ.*

This term "head" is consistently misunderstood today. First, let us understand that the term is non-hierarchical. Paul is elucidating the point of origin for each. His purpose is to address disorder in worship within the Church. Were he setting up a hierarchy, God would not be listed last. He simply says the origin or source of man is Christ, and we know Christ was involved in the creating and forming for scripture says, *Let us make man.* And John 1:3 likewise affirms this point. Already we have established that the woman was taken out of man, and that Jesus came in His incarnate form from the Father. (He was, in the beginning, with the Father; but in the form of a human for the mission of redemption.) Paul, then, is showing this order from a relational perspective not hierarchy.

From verses 4-15, Paul discusses their own traditions and practices, not the ones he delivered to them. We can conclude this based on verse 16: *But if one is inclined to be contentious, we have no other practice, nor have the churches of God. But in giving this instruction, I do not praise you because you come together not for the better but for the worse.* Now, let us examine the cultural context of that which Paul says is not actively practiced: head coverings.

Paul is speaking of the literal, physical head of a man and a woman. In some local congregations of Jews, the priests were required to have a head covering. The Woman's Bible suggests that on Jewish traditions the priests were required to have a head covering.[7] Those traditions are recorded in Exodus 28:4, 37-38; 29:6,9; 39:28,31; and Leviticus 8:9. Kluame Spake writes in *You are Acceptable to Me* that Jewish men, not Jewish women, covered their heads to worship with a garment called a "*taelith.*"[8] Some men wore a *taelith* all the time. In contemporary culture, orthodox Jewish males wear head shawls during prayer. Greek and Roman males also usually prayed with covered heads except before the Father of the gods and before a deity known as "Glory." Thus, head coverings are common to the culture of the geographical area, Christian and Gentile.[9] Spake also asserts that Jewish women wore their hair bound up in public because unbound hair was almost considered as nudity, or immorality.[10] In the Greek Christian church, men who covered their heads with a *taelith* would be indicating that Christ was not as divine as a Greek god. He would "dishonor his own head" or his source, Christ, by praying to God with his head covered. Thus, we can plainly see that covered heads in worship meant different things to different groups. [11]

In order to fully understand the verses here that address women, we must outline the cultural attitude towards women. First, the time between the Old and New Testaments is depicted by moral decay. During the four centuries that elapsed, the Jews were subject to the rulership of people who did not know God. The seventy years of Babylonian Captivity and their primary interaction with pagan natives left its impact on Jewish laws and customs even though during that time span there was consistent worship of God.

Within the worship of God, sexual gratification became a part of the central focus. This demanded the devaluation of women. While in Babylon, women were required to enter the temple and to prostrate themselves in the presence of idols. It was considered a merit for parents to devote their daughters to a life of sexual commerce for the enrichment of the sacred coffers. Babylon the Great opened the market for the sale of women. This then led to the classification of women into five categories.[12]

The first class of women was wives. They were totally confined and had little or no exposure to the world beyond their homes. Their purpose was to birth Greek citizens. They had no rights or privileges. They were the sole property of their husbands. They could not even sit at the table of their masters.

The second class of women was the Hetarirai. They were the only free women in Athens. They were the intellectuals who delivered public address, taught rhetoric, elocution, and founded schools of philosophy. These women associated with men in public and had tremendous influence in the affairs of state. Married men would take these women to social events, not their own wives.

The third class is called the Auletride, or flute players. They were usually imported slaves. They were the entertainers at banquets, and they could be sold at any time during their performance.

The fourth class consisted of the concubines. They too were purchased slaves who became a part of the household with the knowledge of the fact that there was a lawful wife.

The fifth class of women was the Dicterides. They were state prostitutes who rarely came out during the day.

Now, in reference to our scripture, while women did not use a *taelith*, Jewish and Gentile women did veil themselves.[13] Some Rabbis demanded a man divorce his wife if she was seen in public unveiled. In some pagan ceremonies women would discard their veils as a sign of freedom from their oftentimes oppressive husbands.

Verse six, then should be examined. Here, we must understand that if a woman's head was shaved, it was a mark of disgrace. The shaving of a woman's head was used as punishment and reprisal. Therefore, if a woman had a shaven head, Paul suggests she cover it. Furthermore, women who did not wear veils and who had bald heads or short hair could be mistaken for prostitutes or entertainers. The Hetariai wore their hair shorter than the men. As a final blow to the value of women, the Greeks held that woman was created from a substance inferior to that of man.[14] The philosophers held that woman could never be equal with man in moral or spiritual qualities and was, therefore, unworthy to be his true companion.[15] Thus, as you can surmise, it is necessary that there be an understanding of the customs, values, and culture of the times in order to fully understand Paul. Without such study, it is easily plausible to misappropriate the truth.

In verse 7, Paul is saying to the men that since you are in the image of God, you should not have your head veiled. Woman is in the image of man (when God formed woman, she was taken out of man) - she reflects both God and man. In the beginning when God created man and woman they both were in His image and likeness. When God formed man from the ground, he reflected God. When God took woman out of man, she reflects man. (*She is bone of my bone and flesh of my flesh. She shall be called woman because she was taken out of man.*) Verse 8 reaffirms that woman was created for man because we know from Genesis 2: God had judged that man needed help to carry out God's commands to tend the garden and to keep or protect it. Woman was made for man as an equal partner to accomplish the purpose of God. Man alone (in his separation) could not comply with God's command. Verse 10 finishes by saying woman "should have a symbol of authority on her head" because of the angels. The Greek New Testament reads, *A woman should have power over her head (physical head) because of the angels.* The word "power" is *exousia*, which means a freedom of choice. Therefore, the verse says that a woman should have the freedom of choice to cover or uncover her head, and she should not be judged or categorized because of her choice. Additional scriptures using the same language, *power over*, include: Luke 9:1 *Power and authority over demons*; Luke 10:19 *Authority over all the power of the enemy*; Revelation 2:26 *Power over the nations*; Revelation 6:8 *Power over the fourth part of the earth?*; Revelation 14:18 *Power over fire*; and Revelation 16:9 *Power over these plagues.*

Some writers have inferred that to the Greeks, the uncovered head of the woman made her a seduction to evil spirits. They were a very superstitious people. However, the word "angel" also means "messenger." Possibly, one observing a woman with an uncovered head would judge her not to be virtuous, suitable for marriage. Such a judgement could discredit the woman.

Verse 11 depicts the mutuality of male and female in the scripture. Man and woman are interdependent on one another. They together reflect the image of God. Verse 12 reveals that man and woman find their origin in one another realizing that all comes from God the creator and former of each person. Galatians 3:28 declares that in Christ there are not natural distinctions made based on calling and service to God.

If we were writing an epistle today to show the difference between proper Christian deportment and culture, those who would read our work void of understanding the times in which we live might also make laws that would not reflect the true meaning of what we were addressing.

THREE ORDERS OF RELATIONSHIPS

1. Relationship of husband and wife. (Reciprocity)

2. Relationship of children to parents. Children are to obey your parents in the Lord.

3. Relationship of servants to masters. Slaves are to obey masters according to the flesh.

T Y P E S O F S U B M I S S I O N

- ◆ Cultural Submission

- ◆ Traditional Submission

- ◆ Contemporary Submission

- ◆ Biblical Submission

DISCUSSION

1. Discuss your concept of submission and the ways it agrees or disagrees with the material in this section.

2. Give some examples of the misuse of the concept of submission in the home.

3. Discuss examples of civil disobedience to unjust laws.

4. How are Christians to submit to "those in authority?"

5. When is submission not justified?

Chapter Eight Endnotes

[1] Susan C. Hyatt, *In The Spirit We're Equal: The Spirit, The Bible, and Women - A Revival Perspective* (Dallas, Texas: Hyatt International Ministries, 1998) pp. 256-257.

[2] Katherine Bushnell, *God's Word to Women - "Lesson 38: What Does 'Subjection Mean'?"* (North Collins, N.Y.: Ray B. Munson, 1923) para. 292-299.

[3] Ibid.

[4] C. Kroeger, "God's Purpose in the Midst of Human Sin," *Women Abuse and the Bible",* ed. C. Kroeger and J. Beck (Baker: Baker, 1996) pp.211.

[5] Patricia Gundry, *Neither Slave Nor Free* (New York: Harper and Row, 1987) pp.47.

[6] John Temple Bristow, *What Paul Really Said About Women* (New York: Harper and Row, 1988) pp.47.

[7] Catherine Clark Kroeger, Mary Evans, and Elaine Storkey, *Study Bible For Women* (Grand Rapids, Michigan: Baker Books, 1995) pp.344.

[8] Kluame Spake, *You Are Acceptable To Me*, pp.79.

[9] Fred Wright, *Manners and Customs of Bible Lands* (Chicago: Moody Press, 1953) pp.96.

[10] Kluame Spake, *You Are Acceptable To Me*, pp.80.

[11] George M. Lamsa, *New Testament Commentary* (Philadelphia: A. J. Holman Company, 1945) pp.272.

[12] Lee Ann Starr, *The Bible Status of Woman* (Zarephath, N.J.: Pillar of Fire, 1955), pp. 161-163.

[13] James M. Freeman, *Manners And Customs of the Bible* (Plainfield, N.J.: Logos International, 1972), p.32.

[14] Judith Romney Wegner, *Chattel or Person?* (New York: Oxford University Press, 1988), p. 193.

[15] Rosemary Agonito, *History of Ideas on Woman* (New York: Berkley Publishing Group, 1977), pp 40-54.

ONE EXAMPLE OF DEALING WITH DIFFICULT SCRIPTURES

9

Part of the controversy surrounding the issue of gender is to be found in several epistles. The views regarding these Scriptures range from the traditional view that women should not exercise authority over or teach men to the view of the full equality of men and women in the Church. In this section, we shall explore a possible approach to I Timothy 2:12 which has served as a significant source of debate. We will address the cultural context surrounding the epistle.

> *I do not permit a woman to teach or to have authority over a man; she must be silent. I Timothy 2:12*

I Timothy - Background and purpose

On Paul's fourth missionary journey, he instructs Timothy to care for the Church at Ephesus (I Timothy1:3).

Paul addresses the following issues:

> ➤ To refute false teachings (I Timothy 1:3-7; 4:1-8;6:3-5,20, 21)

➤ To supervise the affairs of the growing church in worship. (I Timothy 2:1-5)

➤ To appoint qualified church leaders. (I Timothy 3:1-13; 5:17-25)

The major problems facing the church can be summarized as follows:

➤ Gnosticism

➤ Judaism (The Law)

➤ False asceticism (I Timothy 4:1-5)

➤ Prayer in public worship (I Timothy 2:1-8)

➤ Women in public worship (I Timothy 2:9-15)

➤ Qualification for church offices (I Timothy 3:1-13)

Gnosticism was considered one of the most dangerous heresies of the first two centuries. It appeared about the same time as Christianity, and it was as formidable as Judaism. The basic error of gnosticism, addressed by Paul, can be summarized as follows:

➤ Man's body, which is matter is, therefore, evil. It is to be contrasted with God, who is wholly spirit and, therefore, good.

➤ Salvation is the escape from the body, achieved not by faith in Jesus Christ, but by special knowledge (Greek word of "knowledge is *gnosis*).

➤ The denial of Christ's true humanity. (Christ was thought to be a ghost or a phantom and, therefore, seemed to have a body:

➢ Gnostics disregarded the human body, and they allowed sexual immorality without moral consequences.[1]

Docetism. The other error speculated that the Divine Christ joined the man Jesus at baptism and left Him before he died.)

Women were not allowed access to public or private education. Some daughters of wealthy fathers were privileged to receive some education. Because of the freedom Christianity offered women, many joined the ranks of this new "way" because it liberated them from oppressive customs and traditions.

Judaism was oppressive to women.[2] The Rabbis did not permit women to read the Torah or to be exposed to instruction.[3] The morning service of Judaism still retains the ancient thanksgiving: "Blessed art thou, O Lord our God, King of the universe, who hast not made me a woman."[4]

Paul's letter to Timothy addressed the whole social scheme. The issue of ancient mythology was addressed. It was believed that the original creator of the universe was a goddess and that other gods came from her.[5] The Egyptian goddess Isis, Diana, and Artemis were among them. It was believed that Adam and Eve came from a goddess and that the whole creation story was reversed. In essence, saying that the man came from the woman. So, Paul advised Timothy to have nothing to do with old fables and wives tales that further propagated ancient myths.

We know that Paul says women should learn in quietness and full submission in I Timothy 2:. What we don't often hear is that men and young boys were instructed to be in total submission and quietness as well while being taught. They were not allowed to ask questions publicly. Paul, then, in response to an inquiry, advises Timothy to let the women learn <u>precisely like the men</u>. As you can see, the issue of quietness and submission was instruction for both men and women. The word "quietness" (*hesuchios*) indicates tranquility arising from within, causing no disturbance to others; i.e., settled down.

Paul encourages Timothy to re-educate people who are coming from other cultures and religious groups. They **all** must learn how to behave in the house of God. They **all** must learn proper foundational teachings. The crux of our study of I Timothy 2:12 is this: Paul says, *I do not permit a woman to teach or have authority over a man. She must be silent. For Adam was formed first, then Eve and Adam was not the one deceived; it was the woman.* The word "authority" is *authentin.* (To claim of ownership, to begin something, to be primarily responsible for a condition or action, to rule or dominate, to claim sovereign authority or usurp the power or right of another). Paul is advising Timothy to instruct the women not to teach that humanity started with Eve, an idea they were deriving from Gnostics. The women were claiming the origination of humanity began with Eve.

Also, it should be noted that the gnostics were opposed to childbearing. They propagated the myth that if a woman had a child she would be bound to the earth. Before she could ascend to heaven she would be required to re-gather the souls of all her children in order to go to the true god. Paul corrects these fables by restating the sequence of the Genesis story. Hence, in reading the scriptures relating to the silence of women and the issue of usurping authority, it appears that Paul was addressing erroneous teachings and gnostic error, rather than restricting the rights of women to learn and to teach.

Chapter Nine Endnotes

[1] F. L. Cross, *The Oxford Dictionary of the Christian Church* (London: Oxford University Press, 1974), pp. 573-574.

[2] Jacob Neusner, *The Mishnah* (Philadelphia: Trinity Press, 1992) pp. 175-195.

[3] James Hastings, *Dictionary of the Apostolic Church* (Edinburgh: T & T Clark, 1926) pp 690.

[4] Ibid.

[5] J. M. Davis, *Dictionary of the Bible* (Grand Rapids: Baker Book House, 1972), p. 185.

One Example Of Dealing With Difficult Scriptures

10

CO-LABORSHIP

The concept of co-laborship was not uncommon in the Old Testament narratives. Common examples that are often overlooked are Abraham and Sarah (Gen. 12-18), Elkanah and Hannah (I Sam. 1:2-22), Rebecca and Isaac (Gen. 25: 20,21,28), and Manoah and his wife (Judg. 13). The focus has often been upon the patriarchs without consideration of the matriarchs who also participated in the work of the covenant.

In the New Testament women assumed authoritative roles in the early churches as prophets and teachers. The references to Phoebe and Priscilla introduce another designation of women as *co-laborers*. Paul used the term "co-laborer" (*synergos*) for those who assisted him in ministry. The term with its equivalent, "hard laborer" (*kopion*) refers to a specific group of people. Paul's traveling group consisted of a number of people who were involved in the work of the ministry (Acts 13: 13:21:8; Phil. 2:25-30; 4:18; Coll. 1:7-8; 4:12-13). The members of Paul's company changed with time and consisted of local leaders and itinerants who may have settled in a particular area for a period of time. Reference is made to both Timothy and Titus (I Thes. 1:1; II Tim. 4:9-13; 20-21: Titus 1:5).

Paul's company of co-laborers assumed a variety of different responsibilities. They carried out apostolic duties to other churches (Titus 1:5; I Cor.4:17; 16:10-11), submitted reports to Paul about the status of churches under his charge (Phil. 4:18; Col. 4:10; I Thes. 3:6), hosted churches in their homes (I Cor. 16:19; Philemon 2: 2 Jn.1), and assisted in the writing of letters (Rom. 16:22; I Thes. 1:1). [1]

Paul made reference to men and women as his co-laborers. He encouraged the recipients of his epistles to honor the work of these workers (Rom. 16:1-2; Eph. 6:21-22; I Cor. 16:16). Paul never requested his readers to honor only men and disregard women. In fact some of the women assumed authoritative functions such as preaching and teaching.[2]

Euodia and Syntyche were two women who were "yokefellows" and who labored with Paul in the gospel (Phil. 4:2-3). Paul declared that these two women "shared with me in the struggle in spreading the good news." The fact that they shared with Paul in the "struggle" gives some indication that these two women worked with great zeal for the spreading of the Gospel in Philippi. Victor Pfitzner suggests that these women had an active role in preaching the gospel.[3] Whatever labor Euodia and Syntyche performed, Paul honored their work the same as that of men such as Clement. He even lists them alongside other "fellow labourers."

Paul makes reference to twenty-seven people among which included six women (seven, if you include Junia) in his extended greeting in the close of the epistle to the Romans (16:1-16). Significant on the list is Aquilla and Priscilla, who along side of Urbane are referred to as "fellow workers." Mary and Persis are two of the women who "bestowed much labor." Paul refers to Typhaena and Tryphosa who "labored in the Lord."

Wayne Gruden explored the commendations of Paul concerning these women. It is his belief that the honor given to them, especially to Euodia and Syntyche, is conclusive evidence to refute the alleged limitations that are set forth in I Timothy 2:12.[4] Whatever the actual function of women, Paul regarded them highly. And in his epistles he regarded them as colaborers which was for Paul a significant term (I Cor. 3:9; 2 Cor. 6:1; 8:23; Phil. 2:25; Col. 4:11; I Thes. 3:2; Phlm. 1:24; 3 Jn. 8).

In our contemporary setting, we will certainly experience more men and women co-laboring together. As we begin to identify giftings and abilities without gender bias, more effective leadership models will evolve. This is now evident in some contemporary ministries where one member of a male/female team has ceased to function either due to death or health restrictions and the other has carried on the ministry most effectively.

Chapter 10 Endnotes

[1]Stanley J. Grenz, *Women in the Church* (Downers Grove: InterVarsity, 1995), p. 84.

[2]Ibid.

[3] Victor C. Pfitzner, *Paul and the Agon Motif:* Traditional Athletic Imagery in the Paulin Literature (Leiden: Brill, 1967), p. 120.

[4] John Piper and Wayne Gruden, eds., Recovering Biblical Manhood and Womanhood: A Response to Evangelical Feminism (Wheaton, Ill.: Crossway, 1991), p.68.

GENDER, RELIGION AND SCIENCE

We live in a society in which the boundaries of influence between social, political and religious disciplines are not always readily identified nor maintained. The social activist is not totally separated from the politician when addressing issues of local or national interest. The politician plays the scientist when publicizing the damage done to our rivers and national forests. And both the politician and social activist cannot always separate their convictions from their religious beliefs-and of course they probably should not!

Concepts about life, death and eternity are foundational religious convictions that have a way of influencing the social and political environment. Social and political issues surrounding abortion, euthanasia and ecology have been influenced by the theological propositions set forth by religion. But the relationship between men and women has always been a socio-political issue with religious reflections. Key questions have always been asked. Are men and women equal? Is sex an appropriate attribute to differentiate the human race, dividing work and social positions into men and women's roles? Are they both equally endowed with equal intellectual abilities? Is it possible that the innate ability of a woman to bear children and a man's relatively greater physical strength a feasible basis for determining social positions?

The possibility that genetic differences between men and women should determine their value and behavior has been an issue of much theological discussion. Positions have ranged from the traditional view or male domination, to an egalitarian position in which women have equal access and opportunity with men. Some religious leaders have openly declared that "women are from Venus" and "men are from Mars" and consequently they should function differently in the home and the Church. Other leaders have labeled the issue of men and women relationship as simply another feminist agenda item. But it is not! It is a creational rights issue with tremendous implications affecting every sphere of human involvement. And perhaps rather than resorting to the objectivity of religion for a resolution of the conflict, it may be advisable to consider the empirical field of science-if science is still empirical.

Gender and Sex

Scholars use the word "sex" to refer to biological characteristic that distinguish men and women. Gender is used to refer to qualities of men and women that are established by the culture (masculinity and femininity).

Gender distinctions, like age and race, is ordered by society. Social hierarchy, occupational opportunities and constraints are reproduced because of gender bias. This has been the basis of the time-dated issue of genetic or biologic determinism-are women inherently inferior to men? Did creation produce a female species that is inherently less endowed intellectually and rationally than the male counterpart? Such questions have been raised in an effort to give credibility to the subordinate social status of women.

We believe that some individuals are born more intelligent and mentally capable than others, but it remains difficult to measure the influence of environment and social conditioning on intelligence and capability. Scientist disagree over how much intelligence and capability arrives with the body at birth and how much is created or influenced by personal decisions and social conditioning. We know that the brain is necessary for intellectual ability and that an individual's capability to function intellectually can be impaired by damage or disease to the brain. But they do not know if the brain creates attitudes such as nurture, love, or tolerance because of social stimulation. For example, we have no research to show that criminals are born and predisposed to do evil, although genetic research by E.O. Wilson (1978) and Dawkins (1976) have claimed that genetic inheritance accounts for such traits as aggression, dominance and selfishness. And such anti-social traits can contribute to criminal activity.

Science, like religion, has searched for some reason to support the existent distinctions or similarities among people. If we accept the premise of creation, the question to be raised is this: If humanity (male and female) is created in the image of God, was that image disproportional? Were the capacities given to the man and woman different? Or was it an equal image with regard to intellectuality, rationality and creativity? Did the creational distinctive rest only in their reproductive capacities? These are critical questions. And the correct answers to these questions will help scientists, churchmen and social philosophers alike to properly address the issues of sex-role assignments in the home, market place and the Church. It will further address the theories and propositions that imply that all women are essentially similar in their emotional make-up and behavior and that all men essentially think and operate the same, irrespective of class, age, race, education, occupation, or marital status.

Men, Women and Behavior

The proposition that the sex of a person is directly responsible for behavior has been addressed in political circles. Lazarsfeld and Rosenberg[1] dispelled the so-called "gender-gap" that has supposedly led to differences in voting responses between men and women. Their research revealed that the so-called "gender-gap" differences in voting on issues did not reflect a sex difference between men and women. They discovered that the voting responses of men and women on issues were not significantly different.

This raises a question: What is the impact of culture or biology on behavior? Harvard scientist E.O. Wilson[2] defines sociobiology as the study of the biological basis of social behavior. Sociobiologists base their conclusions about the relationships that exist between evolution and human behavior on the observations of animal studies. Wilson maintains that there are parallells between the development of human beings and African apes. Furthermore, like Darwin, Wilson postulated that the strongest individuals are the most likely to reproduce and to survive. Thus, nature has bred into humans the desire to reproduce and their behavior is motivated by this desire to survive. Men and women follow reproductive patterns that maximize the continuity of their species.

According to this theory, the genetic code (genetic determinism) has directed the brain and the hormone; therefore, the behavior of men and women is predetermined. The position of men and women in the social order simply reflects the evolutionary selection of the most capable human species. Male aggression and female passivity is seen as an evolutionary response that enables men to procreate with as many females as possible and thereby increase the chance of the survival of the species.

Observation of the behavior of baboons, rhesus, and macaque monkeys has been the basis for the sociobiologists' conclusion that male dominance is ordained by nature. The implication of such conclusion is inevitable: male dominance in society and especially in the political and economic spheres is viewed simply as an extension of this evolutionary patriarchy.[3]

The sociobiologists challenge the contentions of other scientists who explain human behavior as a result of culture and social conditioning. The possibility that human behavior can be learned and conditioned has posed a significant challenge to the concept of genetic predeterminism. There are biological factors that create behavioral differences between men and women. Hormones, brain size and shape, and the biological clock that determines the stages of development in life have all been proposed as factors that influence human social behavior. Reproduction processes and the structure of the body are determined by the genetic makeup of the individual.

The issues involved in this debate are political, social and theological since they influence the degree of equality or inequality of women in society. If the genes have determined that women are always less endowed than men, then the assumption is that class hierarchy and female inequality are inevitable. However, if the influence of culture and social experience upon human behavior and personality is being viewed as paramount, then inequality between the sexes cannot be explained by the process of evolution and genetic determinism.

The Sexual Brain

The size, shape and the interrelationship between the two lobes of the brain have been used to explain intellectual differences between men and women, blacks and whites, and Asians and Europeans. The smaller size of the female brain was thought to account for the differences in intellect between men and women by nineteenth century scientists. However, such claims have been repudiated by contemporary research.[4] Much attention has been given to the research of Norman Geschwind on the difference between men and women based on the "split brain theory."[5] He believes that the two lobes of the male brain work independently and that in the female brain the two lobes interact more. This relationship between the two lobes of the brain is alleged to be the cause of the difference in mathematical ability, judgment, and verbal skills that are supposed to exist between men and women. From this theory it is alleged that men can perform different tasks at the same time and women are capable of performing a single task at a time without confusion. Much of this work is based on animal studies.

Other studies of the brain activity have demonstrated that the relationship between the two lobes can be affected by the social environment and is not a fixed factor based on sex.[6] The "split brain theory" alleges that men are more "left brain" and women are more "right brain" in their respective orientations. However, if the environment and social exposure of the individual influences brain activity, then the alleged inherent sex difference in mathematics, judgment and problem solving of spatial arrangements is a matter of orientation and learning and not simply genetics.

Hormones, Cycles and Behavior

Hormonal differences between the sexes have been used as an explanation for the existing social order and male superiority in certain occupations. Some scientists argue that the genes produce differences in behavior and ability by determining the amount and the activities of the sex hormones.[7] The male hormone "testosterone" is supposed to cause boys to be physically more active and aggressive than girls and therefore accounts for the higher social position of men. Since aggression and physical activity contribute to success in society, men will assume a higher position than women because of their hormonal endowment.

It has been postulated that the female hormones and their cycles prohibit women's productive involvement in public life. Edgar Berman, medical adviser to the late Hubert Humphrey, recommended that women not participate in public affairs because of their "raging hormones."[8] Such a partisan attitude was uncovered by UN ambassador Jean Kirkpatrick who acknowledged that some of the opposition to her appointment was because of her female "temperament."[9]

The relationship between hormones and menstruation has been viewed as an explanation for women's emotional behavior and associated with their intellectual ability or lack of it. However, scientific research has demonstrated that the degree which hormone affect moods and behavior varies from person to person and from month to month in some individuals.[10] Although women experience physical discomfort associated with the cycle, the evidence of hostility, anxiety, and depression that is said to hinder their ability to function in public office is contradictory. Work by Golub demonstrated that women exhibited no differences in their test performances over the course of their menstrual cycles.[11] This is most significant when addressing the alleged variation in performance levels of women because of their monthly cycles. Furthermore, the broad speculation over the genetic superiority of men over women in public office or any occupation has not been substantiated by scientific research.

There exists a wide range of behavior in the daily life of men and women that is not so easily explained by hormonal levels. The dominance of men and the passivity of women is now being viewed as a result of behavioral modification due to social conditioning.[12] That is, the social environment experienced by each individual, regardless of sex, has a tremendous influence upon behavior. In certain Churches, women who are aggressive and assertive are not given the same opportunity as those women who are passive and submissive. The aggressive and assertive women who have entered into the leadership sphere of such Churches have done so by subordinating their strong temperament.

Gender, Personality and Emotions

We commonly experienced phrases such as "just like a man" or "just like a woman" which are used to describe commonly accepted male and female behavior and personality. Such phrases infer what is normal for a man and a woman and those who deviate from these traits are regarded as exceptional.

This tendency at over-categorization is extended into racial groups.[13] All blacks are thought to have the same musical and athletic ability and all Jews are supposed to be ambitious, crafty and avaricious. Categories such as "White music" and "Black music" have been created to express an alleged consistency of musical preferences among racial groups. Such conclusions have obviously been found to be faulty. Social scientist have long been engaged in a battle to demonstrate the distinctive differences in intellectual abilities, preferences and behavior that are exhibited by individuals within the same racial group.

Researchers have focused on the role of social factors such as social class, education and religion in determining how people think and behave. The belief that external social factors shape male and female personality and behavior has received considerable support.[14]

The attitude that men and women are good at different tasks, capacities and activities has tremendous implications in the positions and opportunities they assume in the labor force and family based on sex. The critical questions being posed are these: Are men and women endowed equally in talent, creativity, rationality, or do these traits differ among the sexes? If there are differences, then what causes these differences?

The role of social situations and circumstances on personality development, on motivation and aspiration, and on other qualities has been documented.[15] Men and women have different orientation and perspectives toward justice, morality and nurturing, not because of heredity, but because of their distinct social conditioning. Therefore, it is social orientation, not genetics, that causes women to be more open, communicative and cooperative and a different social orientation that causes men to demonstrate separation, isolation and repression of feeling and impulse.

Arlie Hochschild developed a concept called the "sociology of the emotions," in an effort to explain how culture and social conditioning influences the kind of emotions that should accompany certain social roles.[16] Her research points out that social organizations determine what feelings are acceptable and that people adjust their feelings and emotions to adapt to the demands of the social environment. Hochschild postulated that women are encouraged and even directed by the culture to demonstrate "feminine" feelings such as niceness and sweetness while men are motivated to express "masculine" feelings such as aggressiveness and assertiveness.

The work of Kohn and Schooler and their associates was the first to use a national sample to demonstrate the relationship between work and personality.[17] They discovered that the job affected the individual more than the individual affected the job. Job conditions had a tremendous affect on the self-esteem, motivation and personality of the individual. These results proved what researchers had thought all along: people can change. Moreover, social conditioning can change the individual's personality or reinforce an existing group of personality traits. I have personally experienced this phenomena in certain religious spheres where pastors assume a certain persona because of the expectations and demands of their congregations.

A Woman's Place and a Man's Place

It has not been long since the Want-Ad sections in the local newspaper designated certain jobs as male or female. Even today, the culture assigns a designation of "male" or "female" to a task based on tradition or ideology.[18] This sex typing or sex labeling of certain occupations is the process of assigning "male" or "female" to a task. It influences the choices of men and women and permits or denies access to certain occupations. Nursing, for example, has long been sex typed as a female occupation (Occupations are sex typed when a very large majority of those in them are of one sex). Sex typing ultimately results in the polarization of men and women into different occupations and explains the designation of such occupations as male or female. It explains the stereotyping of women as masculine who venture into "male occupations" and the labeling of male nurses to be effeminate.[19]

What are the dangerous consequences of isolating men and women into separate categories with different statuses? Such polarization results in conflict according to some theories of social change.[20] I personally experienced such conflict during the civil rights movement of the 1960's and the racial discrimination with all of its social implications. Whenever there is an inequality among any group because of being forced into a category there is conflict.

The 1993 U.N. Human Development Report claims that men are still treated better than women in every country of the world.[21] Although women are only about one-third of the global workforce, they reportedly account for two-thirds of total working hours but receive only 10 percent of total income paid.[22] These facts are presented simply to demonstrate the social implications of separate categories with different statuses.

As our society moves from industrialization to post-industrialization, opportunities for women are expanding according to Howard Snyder.[23] This is true in part because physical size and strength are less a factor in an information society. Intellect and ability become paramount in such times. According to Snyder, the major areas to be affected by such changes include education, health, legal structures, politics, communication, and the family.

Snyder cites the following signs of the times:

> Women are starting new businesses and cooperatives worldwide in record numbers.

> About 40 percent of the members of Parliament in both Finland and Norway are women.

> In Russia, a women's political party won a sizeable block of seats in the new parliament, elected in 1993.

> Twenty-three percent of the candidates for Cuba's National Assembly, in the nation's first direct election in 1993, were women.

> A record number of women were elected to the U.S. Congress in 1992, raising the total to a historic fifty-three women serving in the two houses.

> For the first time in history, a woman was elected as speaker of Japan's Lower House of Parliament.

> A woman astronaut helped repair the Hubble space telescope.

> ➢ Women are moving up the ranks and to the front lines in national military establishments.

These trends are significant and represent a tremendous challenge to the gender bias that has existed in many occupations.

Gender, Law and Politics

Laws protect whatever is valuable in a society. Most societies fashion laws to maintain valued traditions and to provide for the preservation of treasured landmarks. Laws also create and maintain a particular type of social order. They are usually a reflection of the dominant group of that society and women have been kept in place by the law.

The Supreme Court rejected every effort to overturn sex-based classification by law from 1860 until 1971 according to Judge Ruth Bader Ginsburg.[24] Those laws involved every area of human existence such as family, social security benefits, health care, employment, and housing. The implications of such a legal history was the inherent antagonism or the lack of importance attached to women's rights and equality during those periods of time.

Some law scholars have argued that the law ought to reflect on the reproductive responsibilities of women and the role they play in parenting.[25] Such laws would guarantee pregnancy leave for women before and after childbirth and guarantee their right to reinstatement in the same job or similar jobs.

There are instances in which laws regulate the roles, responsibilities and privileges of men and women in the home and in the market place. Prior to the Civil Rights Act of 1964, occupational segregation prevented married women from working in certain positions. However, changing views have resulted in a reversal of laws, statues and regulations that sex-typed certain occupations. Newspapers have been prohibited from classifying jobs as "male" or "female" in their help-wanted sections.

The Influence of Culture

The influence of external factors in shaping personality characteristics, skills, and preferences is referred to as the theory of socialization. This theory suggests that cultural and societal views that determine the proper attitudes and behavior for males and females are communicated to children through parents, teachers, relatives, friends, and even the media. Socialization creates specific orientations, preferences and abilities in boys and girls that become the basis for their adult orientation, selection and pursuit of occupations in the future.

Socialization begins in the cradle, where the infants receive different treatment and messages based upon their sex. Boys are dressed in blue and are given toys that reflect a rough and ready play. Girls are dressed in pink and are given dolls. The attitudes regarding proper sex role behaviors that are expressed toward the infant is extended throughout childhood and are internalized by the adult males and females. Socialization is seen as encouraging boys to be strong and aggressive and directing girls to be submissive and passive.

Scientific journals reported volumes of research linking cultural messages and the media. Advertisement in magazine depicted women and girls working in the home or caring for others and exerted a tremendous influence of their later career choices and roles as housewives, mothers, teachers and nurses.[26]

The expectations that parents hold for the future of their children varies depending on their sex.[27] Parents expect their sons to perform better in mathematics than their daughters and such expectations, or the lack of them, are a source of motivation to the child.[28] Parental support and encouragement is a strong motive for success to the developing teenager. However, there are numerous instances where the child chooses an occupation contrary to the expectation of parents. This has led some researchers to question the effect of early cultural influences and motivations and the enduring influence they have on future attitudes and choices of boys and girls.[29] Whether the impact of socialization influences all men and women the same is still a matter of research. Some researchers contend that the socialization process is a lifelong process, continuing long after childhood and influencing the choices of men and women.[30] However, some women who have had traditional sex-role orientation have later gone into non-traditional occupations indicating that re-orientation does occur.

Whose Profession Is It?

Discrimination by sex and the division of labor is an interesting study. Employers have objected to hiring women for jobs that were sex-typed for men while hiring them for jobs in which they would be in subjection to men.[31] Law firms explained their reluctance to hiring female attorneys in anticipation of the objection of their clients.[32] It has been my experience that certain religious denominations refuse to install women as pastors of Churches for fear of the backlash from parishoners.

Sex discrimination in the market place may be fueled by money. Some men expressed fears that women equality would greatly compromise their economic survival. Male physicians and lawyers have expressed a similar attitude. The salaries of women in scientific fields is lower than men's.[33] In my profession of dentistry, women were not always readily accepted as applicants for dental schools.

Professional women of equal credentials, productivity and longevity as men have experienced different rates of promotion. Jonathan Cole discovered that women scientists faced discrimination in promotions.[34] Other researchers found that the unemployment rate for women in science was two to five times higher than for men in the same field with comparable training and experience.[35]

All of this research is intended to demonstrate the social stratification of society and the status of women. It also demonstrates a need to re-evaluate the motive behind such discrimination and to actively take some practical steps to correct such conditions.

Women, Men and the Family

The family has long been the critical area of examining the relationship between men and women. The family has been the primary domain of women. Where men were defined in their relation to their occupation, women were often characterized by their role in the family. Men were the protectors and the breadwinners and women were nurturers and the housekeepers. Researchers have presented some different perspectives on motherhood and division of labor in an effort to bring solution to the numerous perplexing problems of divorce, single parentage, teenage pregnancy and violence. The rise in single parent households headed by women has already demonstrated a new division of motherhood: breadwinner, nurturer, housekeeper, and protector. The unemployment rate of married males has also caused a reversal of "domesticated roles." "Mr. Mom" has become more than a possibility.

The evaluation of mother's role has evoked some significant research. Talcott Parsons conceived the woman's role in the family as nurturing and expressive and that of the man as provider for the general welfare of the family.[36] The idealized family of a nurturing mother and a strong, providing father set the pattern and families were considered to be dysfunctional that deviated from this norm. The cause of children's problem were usually identified with the failure of the mother inside the home or the absence of the mother because of outside work.[37] However, this indictment of mothers for the dysfunction of their children has been challenged. The economic status of the household, the neighborhood environment, the type of employment and even the educational level of the mother are variables that contribute to the mother's behavior and to the children. The focus of the mother as the source of the psychological, emotional, and relational state of the child has led to the mother being labeled as the root cause of problems affecting the child.

Conclusions

There are biologic differences between men and women. These differences are consistently obvious in the reproductive process and in distinct physical characteristics. However, the general categorization of occupations, roles and positions in society, home and the Church based on sex is refuted by scientific research. The belief that men and women differ consistently in their intellectual and practical abilities is contradicted by the data. Even research that attempts to support any gender bias has not gone unchallenged by quality documentation. There remains the practical application of scientific data and the removal of any gender bias in politics, economics and religion.

Discussion

1. Define the concept of gender and its application in the home, society and Church.

2. Make a list of ten sex-typed occupations for men and women.

3. Define genetic determinism.

4. Are men and women generally different in their intellectual and rational abilities?

5. What does the research say about the brain of men and women and their behavior?

6. What is the influence of society in determining what is masculine and what is feminine?

7. List several objections to the capability of women to be politicians, pastors and corporate executives.

8. What conclusions can you draw from this study?

Chapter Eleven Endnotes

[1]Lazarfeld, Paul F., and Morris Rosenberg, eds. *Language of Social Research: A Reader in the Methodology of Social Research* (Glencoe, Ill : Free Press, 1955)

[2]Wilson, Edward O. Sociobiology: *The New Synthesis* (Cambridge: Belknap Press of Harvard University Pres, 1975).

[3]Goldberg, Steven. *The Inevitability of Patriarchy*, 2d ed (New York: Morrow, 1974)

[4]Gould, Stephen J. *The Measure of Man* (New York: Norton, 1981)

[5] Geschwind, Norman. *Language of the Brain* Scientific America 241 (3) (1979): 76-83

[6] Lewontin, R. C., Steven Rose, and Leon Kamin. *Not in Our Genes* (New York: Basic Books, 1973)

[7]Barish, David P. *Sociobiology and Behavior* (New York: Elsevier, 1977)

[8]Berman's Book, The Complete *Chauvinest (1982)* alleged the menopausal women would create confusion in policics (Tavris and Wade, 1984)

[9]Kirkpatrick, Jeane. *Political Women* (New York: Basic Books, 1974).

[10]Hoffman, Joan C. *Biorhythms in Human Reproduction The Not So Steady States* (Signs 7(4) (2982):829-844.

[11]Golub, Sharon. *The Effect of Premenstrual Anxiety and Depression on Cognitive Function*. Paper presented at the Annual Convention of the American Psychological Association, Chicago, 1975.

[12]Maccoby, Eleanor E., and Carol N. Jacklin. *The Psychology of Sex Differences* (Stanford, CA: Stanford University Press, 1974).

[13]Allport, Gordon W. *The Nature of Prejudice* (New York: Addison-Wesley Publishing Company, 1979).

[14]Maccoby, Eleanor E. and Carol N. Jacklin. *Review of Psychology of Sex Differences, Sex Roles* 1(3) (1975):297-301.
  Sherman, Julia A. *On the Psychology of Women: A Survey of Empirical Studies* (Springfield, IL:Charles C. Thomas, 1971)

[15]Murray, Henry A., and Clyde Kluckholm. *Outline of a Conception of Personality.* In Kluckholm and Murray, eds., *Personality in Nature, Society and Culture* (1948, New York: Alfred A. Knopf, 1950)3-32.

[16]Hochschild, Arlie. *A Review of Sex Role Research* in Huber, ed., *Changing Women in a Changing Society* (Chicago: University of Chicago Press, 1973): 249-267
Emotion Work, Feeling Rules and Social Structure (American Journal of Sociology 85(2) (November 1979): 551-595.

[17] Kohn, Melvin, and Carmi Schooler. *Occupational Experience and Psychological Functioning: An Assessment of Reciprocal Effects.* American Socialogical Review 38 (February 1973): 97-118.

[18]Oppenheimer, Valerie Kincaid. *The Sex-Labeling of Jobs.* Industrial Relations 7(1968): 219-234.

[19]Epstein, Cynthia Fuchs. *Woman's Place: Options and Limits in Professional Careers* (Berkeley: University of California Press, 1970).

[20]Coleman, James. *Community Conflict* (Glencoe, IL: Free Press, 1957).

[21]MacFarquhar, Emily *The War Against Women,* U.S. News and World Report, March 28, 1994,49.

[22]Quoted in Frank Feathers, *G-Forces: Reinventing the World* (Toronto: Summerhill Press, 1989), 73.

[23]Snyder, Howard. *Earth Currents* (Nashville: Abingdon Press, 1995), 66.

[24]Ginsburg, Ruth Bader. *Sex Equality and the Constitution.* Tulane Law Review 52(3) (April 1978): 451-475.

[25]Law, Sylvia. *Rethinking Sex and the Constitution.* University of Pennsylvania Law Review 132 (1984): 955-1040.

[26]Goffman, Erving. *Gender Advertisements* (London: Macmillan, 1976).

[27]Maccoby, Eleanor E., and Carol N. Jacklin. *The Psychology of Sex Differences* (Stanford, CA: Stanford University Press, 1974)

[28]Marini, Margaret Mooney. *Sex Typing in Occupational Socialization.* In Reskin, ed., *Sex Segregation in the Workplace* (Washington, D.C.: National Academy Press, 1984): 192-232.

[29]Reskin, Barbara F., ed. *Sex Segregation in the Workplace*: *Trends, Explanations and Remedies.* (Washington, D.D.: National Academy Press, 1984).

[30]Reskin, Barbara Fl, and Heidi Hartmann. *Women' Work, Men's Work: Sex Segregation in the Job* (Washington, D.C.: National Academy Press, 1986)

[31]Strober, Myra Hl, and David Tyack. *Why Do Women Teach and Men Manage? A Report on Research on Schools.* Sings 5(3) (Spring 1980): 494-503.

[32]Epstein, Cynthia Fuchs. *Women in Law.* (New York: Basic Books, 1981b).

[33]Astin, Helen S. *The Woman Doctorate in America.* (New York: Russell Sage Foundation, 1969).

[34]Cole, Jonathan. *Fair Science: Women in the Scientific Community* (New York: Free Press, 1979)

[35]Vetter, Betty M. *Women and Minority Scientists.* Science 1989 (4205)(1975):751.

[36]Parsons, Talcott. *The Social Structure of the Family.* In Anshen, ed., *The Family: Its Function and Destiny* (New York: Harper & Row, 1949): 173-201.

[37] Wylie, Phillip. *Generation of Vipers* (New York: Farrar, Rinehart, 1942).

HISTORICAL DEVELOPMENT OF ATTITUDES REGARDING MEN AND WOMEN

In this section we shall examine some of the historical influences that have shaped contemporary attitudes regarding the relationship between men and women. We shall explore the Scriptures and some of the writings of the apostolic fathers in our quest.

The Exodus Narrative

The crisis events in the liberation of Israel and the formation of the people of God were the Exodus and the giving of the law at Sinai. It is interesting to note that the liberation of Israel from Egypt began with the defiance of women against Pharoah. The mothers refused to obey the decree to kill their newborn sons and instead hid them in the bulrushes (Exod. 1:15-22,2:1-10). Miriam, the sister of Moses, hid him in the bulrushes in hope for him to be found by someone. Pharaoh's daughter discovered the Hebrew child and raised him as her own son in violation of Pharaoh's decree. A female conspiracy took place across ethnic and class lines and became the moment of deliverance for the future liberator of Israel.

Moses, Aaron, and Miriam are presented as leaders of Israel in the Exodus narrative (Exod. 15:20-21; Mic. 6:3-4). Even when Miriam is stricken with leprosy and put outside of the camp for her criticism of Moses, the people of Israel refused to continue on their march without her (Num.12:1-15). Dr. Ellicott supposes that the reference to Miriam's criticism of Moses was not racial nor was it due to the influence which Moses is supposed to have allowed Hobab and other members of Zipporah's family to exercise over him. Dr. Ellicott suggests that the occasion for the complaint was something recent and was connected with the Cushite herself. [1]

When Israel is told to prepare themselves for receiving the law at Sinai, they are instructed to keep from women for three days in order to prepare themselves (Exod. 19:14-15; comp. I Sam. 21:4,5; I Cor. 7:5). It was the general sentiment of antiquity that a ceremonial uncleanness was attached even to sexual intercourse. [2] The statement in no way infers that the people are all males nor does it explicitly reference male sacredness to the abstinence of female sexual contact. To make such an assumption would be to assign a source of ceremonial pollution to women and to exclude them from the assembly of God.

An unwritten law of patriarchy seems to be inferred in the book of Leviticus according to some authors. [3] The laws were given to male heads of family. Females, servants, and other dependents in the patriarchal family received the Law indirectly through their relations with males as fathers, husbands, brothers or kinsmen. [4] The penalty for killing or injuring a female is less drastic than the one incurred for the crime against a male [5] (Lev. 24:17,21). The menstrual function of a woman is viewed as a source of pollution and a woman is polluted for twice as long if she bears a female child than if she bears a male child (Lev. 12:1-5, 15:19-27). The Jubilee year takes into account the release of male slaves and makes no mention of females (Lev. 25:39-41). These references seem to indicate a certain patriarchy in Leviticus, however, there is the possibility that a governmental order had been established without the necessary subordination of women. There is a danger in extracting too much from the Leviticus narrative simply because of the absence of the reference to the females in certain instances.

There is a suggestion to be made concerning the issue of menstruating females (Lev. 15:19-26). The issue of blood represents a significant matter of life and death (Lev. 17:11,14). Blood carries the ongoing life of the species (Jn. 1:13; Acts 17:26). The use of the term for "descent" or "family" was ancient and widespread. The belief in the sanctity of the blood underlies the ban on eating it. The menstruating woman was demonstrating a life and death issue. A similar ceremonial law was instituted for any male having an issue of blood (Lev. 15:1-13). Therefore, no derogatory reference should be attached to menstruating woman as an object of offence. To fully appreciate the merciful provisions of the laws, it is necessary to be aware of the gross superstitions that existed among the ancients about women in this condition and the cruel treatment to which wives and daughters were subjected. It was believed that if a woman in this condition sat under a tree, all its fruit fell off; at her approach the edge of a tool became blunted, copper utensils contracted a fetid smell, meat got sour, and thousand of other things. [6] To restrain the Jews from sharing these superstitions, and from resorting to any acts of human cruelty, as well as for sanitary purposes, the Lawgiver ordained these necessary rules. [7]

The New Testament Narrative

The pattern of the New Testament Church is in some ways a reflection of the exodus community. The New Testament Church was viewed as a prophetic community being delivered from conditions of oppression, servitude, sin and death. However, any hierarchies of gender, servitude, and race were banished in the New Testament mode. Paul writing to the Church at Galatia declared that through baptism in Christ "there is neither slave or free, Jew or Greek, male or female, but all are one in Christ (Gal. 3:28). Circumcision of the flesh under the old covenant, which was restricted only to male, finds its completion in the new covenant in water baptism, a rite open to women and men. The new covenant provided for a breakdown of any socioeconomic, racial and gender barriers. However, this concept of a new creature took on different understandings, as we shall discover later.

The Gospels record a new social economy where women, despite their ethnic background, marital history, spiritual status or health condition, could touch Jesus. The Samaritans, Canaanites, harlots, widows and even women with a menstrual flow of blood could approach Jesus. If there were any illogical conclusions drawn from the Exodus narrative concerning women, they certainly were corrected in the Gospels.

The Gospel narratives reveal the faithfulness of women disciples and the privilege of women being the first witnesses of the resurrection (Matt. 28:1-10; Mk. 16:18; Lk. 24:1-10; Jn. 20:1-18). The traditions following the accounts of the resurrection tend to disallow the implications of the participation of women. Even when Paul writes of his own account of the resurrection, he is very much aware of the decisive apostolic factor of being an eyewitness. Yet when he mentions his own account he begins with Peter and neglects to mention Mary Magdalene and the women disciples (I Cor. 14:4-8). Some may take this simply as a contextual oversight while others may attempt to generate a theology of feminine subordination. I dare say that an omission is not in itself an act of deliberate subordination. Silence on an issue in the apostolic writings does not always indicate negligence. It could signify that the knowledge of such a matter was so common that the apostle thought it not necessary even to mention it.

There has evolved a tendency to develop a Christian theology completely through the source of I Timothy and neglect women as prophetesses, apostles, judges, first witnesses of the resurrection and even leaders such as Phoebe, Thecla, Euodia, Syntyche and others. Such a limited theology has produced a patriarchal model of the Church where men alone have governed. And as such the normal Christian community has been one where wives are in subjection to their husbands, children are in obedience to their parents, and slaves are in total obedience to their masters (Col. 3:22-23; I Tim. 6:1,2; I Pet. 2:18-21). The prohibition of slavery has negated the admonition to slaves. Of course, there is no greater injunction to children than to be in obedience to their parents. However, Christian tradition has neglected the possibility that an emerging faith was attempting to provide an alternative community of equalitarianism between men and women. The developing Christian community was progressively restoring a creational order that could be reflected in the home, the market place and the entire society.

Let us now examine some of the historical documents and writing from the post-apostolic period in our effort to discover the possible influences upon the gender issue.

The Church Fathers

In the second and third centuries, an evolving Episcopal Christianity engaged tremendous conflicts, which sought to fragment its communities and even destroy its very roots. In the process of its defense through theological arguments and creedal statements, Christianity evolved into an Episcopal structure, which claimed to be the heir of the original apostolic community. This evolving faith community began to exclude women from any possible Episcopal office because of the belief that since the original apostles were the first bishops and they were all men, then a continuous historical succession should not include women.

A collection of writings, written near the end of the first and the beginning of the second centuries, in Greek, by authors who were thought to be apostles of Jesus, or at least represented the thinking of the apostles, makes up the compilation entitled "The Church Fathers." The writings are usually addressed to churches, or members of the church, and treat specific needs or problems. They make frequent reference to Scripture, and frequently insist that they are in complete harmony with the Gospel teaching. Our particular interest will be the positions presented by these writings regarding women.

The Greek Fathers

Clement of Alexandria is our first subject. Born in Athens, Greece, Clement studied philosophy and Christianity. He decided to become devout to Christianity. He eventually headed the Catechetical School of Alexandria in Egypt. The time in which Clement lived is marked by extremes, as seen in the Egyptian Gnostics. However, Clement seemed to have a balanced attitude towards life. He allowed women into his lectures and spoke of their equality of nature and capacity for wisdom. [8] The paradox rests in his statements regarding manliness:

> *"Man is strong, active, uncastrated, mature; woman is weak, passive, castrated, immature."* [9]

Origen is known as Clement's successor as head of the catechetical school in Alexandria.[10] He was hailed as being quite brilliant. He sought martyrdom, but was prevented by his mother — she hid his clothes. Origen views of women were rather negative:

> *"What is seen with the eyes of the creator is masculine, and not feminine, for God does not stoop to look upon what is feminine and of the flesh."* [11]

> *"It is not proper for a woman to speak in church, however admirable or holy what she says may be, merely because it comes from female lips."* [12]

Origen presents the female as the antithesis to the divine. He also silences the female voice in the church.

Dionysus, Origen's successor as head of the school in Alexandria, became the Bishop of Alexandria.[13] He held to the Hebrew Law of Ritual Impurity. There were three main causes of impurity: leprosy, dead bodies of certain animals, particularly human corpses, and issue from sexual organs. The last one affected women the most. If a man has an emission of semen outside of intercourse, both are unclean.

The Levitical laws concerning the impurity of women are much more restrictive. When a woman has a menstrual discharge of blood, she is

---

unclean for seven days, or as long as it lasts, whichever is longer. Whomever she touches becomes unclean for a day as does anything she touches. (Lev. 15:23-24, & 31; 20:18; 12:2-5) The woman had far more restrictions on her than the male because of her natural functions, which is understandable in consideration of nomadic travels and the possible lack of water for extra cleaning. In this ancient day, women separated themselves until the menstrual period passed.

This was used against women when it came to having access to participate in church functions or simply to learn the word of God. Dionysus forbade women to enter the Church during menstruation. This implied spiritual impurity, along with a woman's natural cleanliness problems during this time. Women were cut off from receiving communion, and any who did and were found out, were excommunicated. Dionysus wrote:

> "The one who is not entirely pure in soul and body must be stopped from entering the Holy of Holies." [14]

Epiphanius, the Bishop of Cyprus and Salamis, was a strict advocate of monasticism and orthodoxy.[15] His attitude toward women may be reflected in the following statement:

> "The female sex is easily seduced, weak, and without much understanding. The devil seeks to vomit out disorder through women. . . We wish to apply masculine reasoning and destroy the folly of these women." [16]

John Chrysostom was a preacher and was referred to as "golden mouthed" because of his eloquence.[17] His opinion of marriage and women in general is reflected in the following statement:

> "Should you reflect about what is contained in beautiful eyes, in a straight nose, in mouth, in cheeks, you will see that bodily beauty is only a whitewashed tombstone, for inside it is full of filth." [18]

He believed marriage was good only to keep men from "becoming members of a prostitute."[19] His position on male dominance and female subordination is vividly depicted in the following:

> "Since private affairs are part of the human condition, as well as public ones, God has doled them out: all that takes place outside, he has trusted to man, all that is within the house, to woman..... This is an aspect of the divine providence and wisdom, that the one who can conduct great affairs is inadequate or inept in small things, so that the function of woman becomes necessary. For if he had made man able to fulfill the two functions, the feminine sex would have been contemptible. And if he had entrusted the important questions to woman, he would have filled women with mad pride. So, he gave the two functions, neither to the one, to avoid humiliating the other as being useless, nor to both in equal part, lest the two sexes, placed on the same level, should compete and fight, women refusing authority to men."[20]

Cyril of Alexandria was a bishop. A very clear, precise, orthodox, and dogmatic theologian, Cyril also displayed himself as a violent self-righteous, unscrupulous, protagonist of his own perceptions and views. He violently attacked the Jews of Alexandria, forcing thousands from their homes and synagogues.[21] His concept of women was exceedingly low – he felt that women were uneducated and could not understand difficult matters well. This was expressed in the following statement:

> "Somehow, the woman (Mary Magdalene) or the female sex as a whole, is slow in comprehension."[22]

Cyril concludes this because he felt that Mary Magdalene was unintelligent in her slow recognition of the glorified Jesus at the resurrection.[23] Cyril's attitude was challenged by a non-Christian Mathemetician and philosopher of the Neoplatonic school in Alexandria – a woman, Hypatia.[24] This woman was known for her "great eloquence, rare modesty, and beauty," and she attracted a great many students. Unfortunately, a Christian monk dragged her from her chariot into a

Christian church, stripped her naked, cut her throat, and burned her body in pieces.[25]

It is here that I must assert briefly that when our views are not well founded, studied, and documented, and when our views violate God, confusion comes to people. They then do the wrong things, thinking that they do it for God, and they violate His very heart.

The Latin Fathers

Tertullian was the first to make the Latin language a vehicle for theology.[26] We shall consider him along with Ambrose, Jerome, Augustine and Gregory the Great in our quest to uncover the attitudes of historic writers upon our topic.

Tertullian, known as the Father of Latin Theology, assumed a posture similar to the Greek Fathers in his appraisal of women. A prolific writer, he blamed women for bringing sin and death into the world, and consequently, the responsibility for the death of the Son of God:

> *"In pains and anxieties dost thou bear children, woman; and toward thine husband thy inclination, and he lords over thee. And do you not know that you are an Eve?*
>
> *The sentence of God on this sex of yours lives in this age: the guilt must of necessity live too. You are the devil's gateway; you are the unsealer of that forbidden tree: you are the first deserter of the divine law: you are she who persuaded him whom the devil was not valiant enough to attack. You destroyed so easily God's image, man. On account of your desert - that is, death - even the Son of God had to die."[27]*

From this statement women are blamed for bringing sin and death into the world and the vicarious death of Christ was their provocation.

Ambrose, the bishop of Milan, was most articulate on the subject of virginity and advice to widows. Three tracts of his - On Virginity, On the Training of a Virgin, and Advice to Widows- assert that virginity is preferred over marriage.[28] The believing female loses her sexual identity and is equated to a male. He wrote:

"Whoever does not believe is a woman, and she is still addressed with her physical, sexual designation; for the woman who believes is elevated to male completeness and to a measure of the stature of the fullness of Christ; then she no longer bears the worldly name of her physical sex and is free from the frivolity of youth and the talkativeness of old age."[29]

Ambrosiaster , writing on I Corinthians 11, expressed a decisive subjection of the woman to the man:

"Although man and woman are of the same essence, nevertheless, the man because he is the head of the woman, should be given priority, for he is greater because of his casual nature and his reason, not because of his essence. Thus the woman is inferior to man for she is part of him, because the man is the origin of woman; from that and on account of that the woman is subject to the man, in that she is under his command . . . The man is created in the image of God, but not the woman. . . Because sin began with her, she must wear this sign [the veil]."[30]

Jerome , like many Christian fathers, felt that the two primary purposes of marriage were reproduction and fulfillment of sexual appetite. He encouraged women to embrace the Christian life but forbade their involvement in leadership.[31]

"What do these wretched, sin-laden hussies want! Simon Eagus founded a heretical sect with the support of the harlot, Helena. Nicholas of Antioch, the contriver of everything filthy, directed women's groups. Marcion sent on to Rome before him a woman to infatuate the people for him. Appeles had Philomena as companion for his teaching. Montanus, the proclaimer of impurity, first used Prisa and Maximilla, noble and rich women, to seduce many communities by gold and then disgrace them with heresy...even now the mystery of sin takes effect. The two-timing sex trips everyone up."

Augustine was without question the greatest of the Latin fathers and the most influential.[32] His attitude towards women follows the traditions of the other Latin fathers. He refutes Genesis 1:27 and insists that the image of God is gender specific:

> *"Unless according to that which I have said already, when I was treating of the nature of the human mind, that the woman, together with her husband is the image of God, so that the whole substance may be one image, but when she is referred to separately in her quality as a helpmeet, which regards the woman alone, then she is not the image of God, but, as regards the man alone, he is the image of God as fully and completely as when the woman too is joined with him as one."* [33]

Augustine portrays the subordination of the woman to the man:

> *"Just as the spirit (mens interior) like the masculine understanding, holds subject the appetite of the soul through which we command the members of the body, and justly imposes moderation on its helper, in the same way the man must guide the woman and not let her rule over the man; where that indeed happens, the household is miserable and perverse."*[34]

Gregory the Great assumed a position similar to the other Christian fathers. His sentiments expressed a subordinate relationship of the woman to the man:

> *"In the Holy Scripture woman stands either for the female sex (Gal.4:4) or for weakness, as it is said: A man's spite is preferable to a woman's kindness (Sir 42:14). For every man is called strong and clear of thought, but woman is looked upon as weak or muddled spirit. What then is designated in this passage by the word "woman" but weakness, when it says: Man born of woman? Just as when it is said even more clearly: What measure of strength can he bear in himself who is born from weakness?"*[35]

The value of the writings of the Church Fathers as a witness to early Christianity are of inestimable worth. The influence of these writings upon contemporary thought is also difficult to assess. However, it is sufficient to conclude that there appeared to exist a consistent attitude expressed in their writings concerning the social and spiritual status of women.

Before ending our quest, let us explore for a moment the era of the Reformation. The period of time between 1500-1650 represented an upheaval in nearly every sphere of thought and action.[36] The social stratification of society changed which medieval men had considered ordained by God for all of eternity. Our concern is the social sphere of society of that time where the relationship between men and women was governed by religious thought. We shall briefly examine some aspects of the theology of Luther and Calvin.

Luther. His commentary on Galatians reveals a consistent attitude regarding the home environment:

> "If the woman live chastely, obey her husband, see well to her household, bring up her children godly (which are indeed excellent gifts and holy works); yet are all these nothing in comparison of that righteousness which is before God."[37]

The prevailing attitude of patriarchy seems to be consistent in the writings. In his treatise of Genesis, Luther wrote:

> "This punishment too springs from original sin; and the woman bears it just as unwillingly as she bears those pains and inconveniences which have been placed upon her flesh. The rule remains with the husband, and the wife is compelled to obey him by God's command. He rules the home and the state, wages war, defends his possessions, tills the soil, builds, plants, etc. The woman, on the other hand, is like a nail driven in a wall. She sits at home....the wife should stay at home and looks after the affairs of the household as one who has been deprived of the ability of

*administering those affairs that are outside and concern the state.....In
this way Eve is punished."* [38]

The social stratification of society based upon gender seemed to prevail
with the exclusion of women from significant roles except in the home.
Even Luther's own marriage to Catherine von Bora, a significant step
for the evangelical cause and the clergy, demonstrated the restricted
domain of the woman in society.[39] Luther was respectful of his "Kette"
whom he jokingly called "My Rib."[40] She was a most efficient
householder and managed the affairs of the home so well that Luther
was moderately well off at his death.[41]

Calvin. The basis of Calvin's theological system was his doctrine of the
absolute authority of God as eternal lawgiver and judge whose will is
law. Therefore, man can be saved only be direct divine intervention.
His views on marriage and the social status of women is reflected in the
following statements:

> *"The woman derives her origin from the man; she is therefore inferior
> in rank. On this account all women are born, that they may acknowledge
> themselves inferior in consequence of the superiority of the male sex.
> Let the woman be satisfied with her state of subjection, and not take it
> amiss that she is made inferior to the more distinguished sex. This
> more 'distinguished sex' alone is responsible for the office of teaching
> which is a superiority in the Church and if the woman is under
> subjection, she is, consequently, prohibited from authority to teach in
> public."* [42]

These brief statements reflect a consistency of thought and practice and
offer support to the premise that the historical writings have provided
a tremendous resource of influence. Let it be said that no effort should
be made to demean nor exalt the writers in their own quest for
knowledge and understanding of divine revelation.

Development of Contemporary Views

As we continue to explore the development of attitudes regarding the relationship between men and women, let us focus upon some of the contemporary religious thought. Our concern is not simply limited to religious thought for we cannot overemphasize the influence of religious attitude upon society. The chief reason is that religion stands for more than faith. It is the pivotal factor in the cultural tradition of a group. Christianity is so very much interrelated with western civilization that at times many of our missionaries exported western civilization and the Bible as their message to other nations. Principles of cross cultural communication are so vividly depicted by Marvin Mayers in his book entitled *Christianity Confronts Culture* in which he states: "Biblical Christianity is a dynamic process born in a change setting, and since it introduces change in the life of individuals and society, it resists being bound by the narrow ethnocentrism."[43] Sects of Christianity have become tied into subcultural and national groups. It is not unusual that a local church becomes the defender of a race, a nation, a people and even a culture. This has happened because religious groups often find in their faith and doctrine justification for the secular practices of their group regardless of the race or ethnic origin. Christian groups have also greatly influenced attitudes regarding the relationship between men and women in the Church, home and the market place.

Gordon Allport in his classic study of the roots of discrimination claims that the process of over-categorization of a whole group without giving attention to individual differences is a common basis of prejudice.[44] The process of categorization causes us to form large classes and clusters.[45] When women are viewed as a wholly different species from men, usually an inferior species, then primary and secondary sex differences are greatly exaggerated and are inflated into imaginary distinctions that justify discrimination.[46] Dr. Allport makes his point quite clear by a quote from Lord Chesterfield to his son:

"Women, then, are only children of a larger growth; they have an entertaining tattle, and sometimes wit; but for solid reasoning good sense, I never knew in my life one that had it, or who reasoned or acted

consequentially for four and twenty hours together.....A man of sense only trifles with them, plays with them, humors and flatters them, as he does a sprightly, forward child; but he neither consults them about, nor trusts them with serious matters; though he often makes them believe that he does both; which is the thing in the world that they are most proud of..."[47]

When such reasoning is supported by religious thought, it becomes the basis for unlimited distinctions between men and women.

With the understanding of the powerful influence exerted by religious thought upon the behavior and attitudes of a society, let us turn our attention to several contemporary views regarding relationships between men and women.

Bonnidell Clouse and Robert G. Clouse edited a splendid work entitled *Women in Ministry* in which the gender debate is narrowed down into four views: 1) traditional, 2) male leadership, 3) plural ministry, and 4) egalitarian.[48] Each view is graciously presented by several contributors and focuses upon several basic Scriptural references that have been the nidus of much controversy: 1) I Corinthians 11:2-16 (*The head of the woman is the man*); 2) I Corinthians 14:34 (*Let your women keep silent in the church*); 3) Galatians 3:28 (*There is neither ......male nor female, for you are all one in Christ Jesus*); and 4) I Timothy 2:11-12 (*But I suffer not a woman to teach, nor to usurp authority over a man*).[49] It is amazing to see how each of the different contributors support their views of the same Scriptural reference. Robert Culver presents a traditional view that forbids women from teaching or exercising authority over men.[50] Alvera Mickelsen argues for the full equality of men and women in the government of the church.[51] Walter Liefeld brings forth a view of plurality.[52] And Susan Foh defends a view which allows women to teach but not to occupy any position of authority.[53]

It becomes apparent that the contemporary views of the gender issue are varied. It does appear that the various treatments of the New Testament Epistles are in themselves influenced by some of the historical writings. And the historical writings themselves were influenced by various understandings of the Genesis story. The order of creation, the deception of Eve and the dimensions of the curse weighed heavily upon most. For that reason, it may be necessary to re-examine Genesis, the source of much of the New Testament revelation on the gender issue, in an effort to gain resolution. This we will do in another section.

CONCLUDING REMARKS

Theology can greatly influence our attitudes and operational behavior. In this section we have explored the various historical writings that have shaped the contemporary concepts of patriarchy and female subordination. The excluding of women from positions of authority seemed to have been influenced by various understandings of the Genesis story. Even though the order of creation, the deception of Eve and the dimensions of the curse do not in themselves imply the inferiority of the woman, the writings explored in this section seemed to present opinions contrary to the Biblical text and scientific research.

It is to be expected that such opinions may have contributed to the omission of the significant contributions of women from the historical writings. Lifefield and Tucker uncovered several women who made significant contributions:

Proba - known for her outstanding literary work of using poetry with Gospel stories.

Marcella - the foremost Bible interpreter of the 4th Century.

Fabiola - founder of the first Christian hospital in Europe.

Paula - a major linguistic contributor to the translation of the Vulgate Bible.

Marcrina - exerted a tremendous impact on non-Christians in Asia Minor through her pioneering of a monastery, a hospital, and a Christian teaching and social service center.

Pulceria - recognized by Pope Leo 1st for her contributions to the Council of Chalecedon and for her vital theological arguments against Nestorian and Eutychean heresies.

St. Thelca - a missionary associate of Paul who exerted tremendous apostolic influence.[54]

Christianity provided for the emancipation of women. During the Apostolic and post-Apostolic periods, women held offices of presbyters and deacons. However, it is interesting to note that within 100 years after the Apostolic times that there was an obvious omission of the contributions of women in church history. Lee Ann Starr suggests that during the latter part of the first, and also during the second century, a strong antipathy developed against the public functioning of women in the church.[55] Such a feeling, according to Starr, resulted in a tampering with the Sacred Text. This was especially noticeable in passages effecting women.

Many of the Ecumenical bodies and councils passed legislations that prohibited women from serving in certain leadership positions. For example, the Council of Laodicea (32 A.D.) prohibited women from serving as priest or presiding over churches; the Fourth Synod of Carthage (398 A.D.) excluded women from teaching men in an assembly, and the Synod of Orange (441 A.D.) forbade the ordination of women as deacons.[56]

From these writings and the prevailing attitudes toward women today, it is clear that Christianity is not simply a reflection of the teachings of Jesus and the Apostles but is a mixture of human philosophies, Judaism, and historical thought. We should seek to separate true Christianity from these unfortunate additions which have served to remove women from their place of honor and respect. We should also re-examine their agreement with the teaching of Scriptures.

CHAPTER TWELVE ENDNOTES

[1] C. J. Ellicott, An *Old Testament Commentary for English Readers* (London: Cassell and Company, 1901), p.515.

[2] Ibid., p.258

[3] Phyllis Bird, *Images of Women in the Old Testament, in Religion and Sexism*: Images of Women in the Jewish and Christian Tradition, ed. R. Ruether (New York: Simon and Schuster, 1974), p.48-57.

[4] Ibid.

[5] Rosemary Radford Ruether, *Women-Church:* Theology and Practice (New York: Harper and Row, 1985), p.44.

[6] C. J. Ellicott, An *Old Testament Commentary for English Readers* (London: Cassell and Company, 1901), p.404

[7] Ibid.

[8] Stromateis 4, 8, and 9.

[9] Clement of Alexandria, Paedagogus 3.3

[10] Kenneth Scott Latourette, *A History of Christianity*, Volume I (New York: Harper and Row, 1975), p.148-151.

[11] Origen, *Selecta in Exodus XVIII.17, Migne, Patrologia Graeca*, Vol. 12, cols. 296f.

[12] Origen, quoted in Leonard Swidler, *Biblical Affirmations of Women* (Philadelphia: Westminister Press, 1979), p.342.

[13] John R. Willis, *A History of Christian Thought* (New York: Exposition Press, 1976), p.209.

[14] Dionysus of Alexandria, *Canonical Epistle*, Ch. 2, Migne, Patrolegia Graeca, Vol. 10, cols. 1282.

[15] Epiphanius, quoted in Swidler, *Biblical Affirmations of Women*, Ibid. P. 343.

[16]Epiphanius, *Adversus Collyridianos*, Migne, *Patrologia Graeca*, Vol. 42, cols. 740f.

[17]Kenneth Scott Latourette, *A History of Christianity*, Vol. I (New York: Harper and Row, 1975), p.98-99.

[18]John Chrysostom, *Letter to Theodora*, Ch. 14, Sources Chreriennes, *Vol. 117, p.167.*

[19]John Chrysotom, *On Virginity*, Ch. 25, *Sources Chreriennes*, Vol. 125, p. 175.

[20]John Chrysostom, *On the One Marriage, Sources Chretiennes*, Vol. 138, p. 183: Homily *Quales ducendae sint uxores*, in *Opera*, Vol. 3, p. 260f.

[21]G. P. Fisher, *History of Christian Doctrine* (Edinburgh: T and T Clark, 1927), p. 152.

[22]Cyril of Alexandria, *Migne, Patrologia Graeca*, Vol. 74, col. 689.

[23]Leonard Swidler, *Biblical Affirmations of Woman* (Philadelphia: Westminster Press, 1979). P.345.

[24]Ibid.

[25]Ibid.

[26]G. P. Fisher, *History of Christian Doctrine* (Edinburgh: T and T Clark, 1927), p. 38.

[27]Tertullian, *De cultu feminarum 1.1, The Fathers of the Church*, Vol. 40, p. 117f.

[28]John R. Willis, *A History of Christian Thought* (New York: Exposition Press, 1976), p.297.

[29]Ambrose, *Expositio evangelili secondum Lucam*, liber X, n161, Migne, *Patrologia Latina*, Vol. 15, col. 1844.

[30]Ambrosiaster, Migne, *Patrologia Latina*, Vol. 17, col.253.

[31]Migne, *Patrologia Latina*, Vol. 30, col. 732.

[32]Justo Gonzalez, *The Story of Christianity* (San Francisco: Harper, 1984), p208-216.

[33] Augustine, *De Trinitate*, 7.7,10.

[34] Augustine, Migne, *Patrologia Latine*, Vol. 34, col. 205.

[35] Gregory, Migne, *Patrologia Latina*, Vol. 75, cols. 982f.

[36] Harold J. Grimm, *The Reformation Era* (New York: Macmillan Publishing, 1973),
pp.5-41.

[37] Martin Luther, *A Commentary on St. Paul's Epistle to the Galatians* (London: James Clark and Co., 1575), p.342.

[38] Martin Luther, *Lectures on Genesis*, 3, 16, quoted by Dr. Kluane Spake, *You Are Acceptable to Me* (Tamuning, Gu.: Jubilee Church, 1991), p. 182.

[39] Harold J. Grimm, *The Reformation Era* (New York: Macmillan Publishing, 1973), pp.144-145.

[40] Ibid.

[41] Ibid.

[42] Margaret E. Howe, *Women and Church Leadership* (Grand Rapids: Zondervan Publishing), p. 62.

[43] Marvin K. Mayers, *Christianity Confronts Culture* (Grand Rapids: Zondervan, 1987).

[44] Gordon W. Allport, *The Nature of Prejudice* (New York: Addison-Wesley Publishing, 1954)

[45] Ibid. p.20.

[46] Ibid. p.33.

[47] C. Strachey (Ed.). *The Letters of the Earl of Chesterfield to his Son* (New York: G.P. Putnam's Sons, 1925, Vol. I. 261); quoted in Gordon Allport, *The Nature of Prejudice* (New York: Addison-Weslry Publishing, 1954), p.34.

[48] Bonnidell Clouse and Robert G. Clouse, *Women in Ministry* (Downers Grove: Intervarsity Press, 1989)

[49] Ibid.

[50]Ibid.

[51]Ibid.

[52]Ibid.

[53]Ibid.

[54] Ruth A. Tucker ad Walter Liefield, *Daughters of the Church: Women and Ministry From New Testament Times to the Present* (Grand Rapids: Zondervan, 1987), pp. 102, 117-120.

[55] Lee Ann Starr, *The Bible Status of Woman* (Zarephath, N.J.: Pillar of Fire, 1955) p. 285.

[56] Ibid., p. 355

13

PRIESTHOOD

While our topic is the priesthood, it is important to establish a principle of Biblical interpretation. The Bible is a progressive revelation of God and His dealings with people. From the book of Genesis to the book of Revelation, there is a gradual unfolding of truth. Augustine stated that the New Testament is concealed in the Old Testament and the Old Testament is revealed in the New Testament. God, who is the source of all truth, communicated to people, stage by stage, as they were able to digest it, an increasing measure of knowledge about Himself.[1] Types, shadows, and symbols in the Old Testament find their fulfillment or "realization" in the New Testament. Moses the servant is succeeded by Jesus the Son. Moses' Law finds it fulfillment in Christ's law, which incorporates the essence of the law of Moses. Nationalism yields to universalism. The Passover surrenders its place to the Lord's Supper. The "blood of bulls and goats" are no longer sufficient in the presence of the "better sacrifice of Himself." The earthly Jerusalem stands in contrast to the "Jerusalem which is above." The Levitical priesthood, like the Mosaic law, served its temporary purpose. The privilege of covenant are no longer confined to a single nation. Every believer, as such, is a priest of God.

The principle of continuity/discontinuity characterizes this progressive revelation as it unfolds from the Old Testament to the New Testament. Some practices and institutions that were prominent in the Old

Testament do not find a place under the new covenant. For example, sacrifices and cleansing regulations are no longer literally binding because they are a shadow of the work of Christ (Col. 2:13-17; Heb. 9:8-10, 10:1-18). But there are some Old Testament practices and institutions that appear under the new covenant in a modified fashion. Worship continues but it is no longer limited to a "place" but to "wherever" (Deut. 12:11; John 4:21; Matt. 18:20). The temple continues but not the "temples made by hands." The priesthood continues but it is modified. And it is this concept of "priesthood" that I wish to explore, both in its historical and contemporary context.

Under the old covenant, the Jewish priesthood held a peculiar relation to God as the representatives of the whole nation. Even though the whole community was regarded as a "kingdom of priests" and a "holy nation," the sons of Levi were set apart as delegates of the people to offer sacrifices and to make atonement. The Levites were, in a sense, ordained by the whole congregation. The "children of Israel," it is said, "shall put their hands upon the Levites." The nation delegated to a single tribe the priestly functions that belong properly to itself as a whole.[2] And as such, the priesthood was "tribal-specific" (Levi), "gender-specific" (males only), and "age-specific" (age twenty-five to fifty). No physical blemish was permitted of a priest such as a flat nose, brokenfoot, brokenhand, crookback, a dwarf, or a blemish in his eye (Leviticus 22:17-20).

The concept of a "priestly tribe" and a "priestly nation" must be understood in the context of divine revelation. Under the Mosaic dispensation, the priestly tribe held a peculiar relation to God only as a representative of the whole nation. As delegates of the nation, the Levitical tribe offered sacrifice and made atonement. In this sense, the priestly tribe served a mediatorial or sacerdotal function. However, the entire nation was a "kingdom of priest" called to reconcile other nations unto God (Exod.19.6). As such, Israel was to be a representative of divine revelation before other nations. And because "Unto them were committed the oracles of God," this priestly tribe was given special responsibilities in their delegation as a mediatorial people.

The Levitical priesthood, like the Mosaic law, served a temporary purpose (Gal.3.19-29). The period of childhood had passed, and the Church of God had arrived at a mature age. The covenant community now assumed their priestly functions (I Pet.2.5, 9; Rev. 1.6; 5.10; 20.6). The privileges of the covenant were no longer confined to a single nation and neither were the priestly functions limited to unblemished male Levites of a specific age (Joel 2.28-32; Acts 2.17-18,39; 10.34-35). Every member of the redeemed community was a priest unto God and authorized to offer "spiritual sacrifices, acceptable to God by Jesus Christ."

The influence of this concept of a universal priesthood had tremendous social implications. This conception of the Church was instrumental in the emancipation of the oppressed and the degraded. It confronted the barriers of class (Gal. 3.14,28,5.6; Eph. 2.13-16; Col. 3.10-11). The concept of a universal priesthood represented a modification of the hierarchical system. All believers, male and female, regardless of their age and physical condition, were legitimate priests and authorize to offer "spiritual sacrifices" unto God. The only priests under the Gospel, designated as such in the New Testament, are the saints.

From a practical standpoint, the male priesthood has been modified to include females. And in a community or a home, the priests represent all who have been redeemed by the blood of Christ. No Christian under the Gospel is authorized to serve as a mediator for another Christian. Even the priestly functions and privileges of the Christian people are never transferred or even delegated to their leaders. Spiritual leaders may be regarded as the mouthpieces or the representatives of a priestly race. However, as long as the leaders are regarded as originating from the priesthood of the whole body, the teaching of the Apostles has not been directly violated.

Redemptive equality presupposes that the benefits of covenant are offered to all believers, regardless of race, creed, tongues, socioeconomic status, gender, or age. The focus of the Reformers was an appeal to the Bible, not tradition or culture, as the focus of authority. And their three principles used in establishing this new focus were sola scriptura (Scripture alone), sola fide (faith alone), and the priesthood of all believers.

Sola fide expounded the biblical truth that salvation is by grace through faith. This delivered the believers from the burden of salvation by works. Of course the practical implications of redemptive equality for men and women in a stratified society still remains a controversial issue. Are men and women equal? If so, how is it to be displayed in society?

Sola scriptura proposes that the bible rather than tradition of culture is the authority for faith and practice. But it appears today, that authority is not always derived from scripture but from interpretation of Scripture. And the crisis of our discussion is based on the fact that interpretation continues to be mixed with a hierarchical worldview, the influence of Greek culture, and the obvious biases against women in government.

The priesthood of believers is the proposition of equality of all believers. However, the issue of equality is compounded when we address the matter of function or "governmental distinctions." That is, are there some priests that still must be silent and in submission to other priests? Is universal priesthood divided into a male and female gender stream with each stream having separate and distinctively different privileges? If there is such an understanding, then the practical outworking of such a concept would be for a household of priests (redeemed woman and children) to function under a high priest (redeemed husband and father). This is the practical and erroneous implication of the concept of a universal priesthood because of a hierarchical understanding of "head" or "headship."(I Cor. 11.2-16; Eph. 4.15,23; 5.21-33; Col. 1.18; 2.10,18)

Because the term "head" is viewed erroneously as "authority over" or "leadership," priesthood in the church and the home is confronted with a chain-of-command and a patriarchal authority structure. And because of this, the concept of head often comes in conflict with the obvious presence of gifts, talents, abilities, and callings that are evident in women.

That is, ecclesiastical positions are often denied to people with true ecclesiastical authority.

The Greek word *kephale* carries no chain-of-command meaning or hierarchical significance. [3] Instead, the word *kephale* means "source of life" (in creation) which is a meaning totally different from authority. Paul's use of the word *kephale* meant that the man was the source of the woman in creation, woman is the source of man in procreation, and Christ is the Source of Life for all humanity.

Discoveries about *kephale* have helped to clarify the concept of a universal priesthood and the governmental implications in the church and the home. At times, the Hebrew word *archon* (ruler, commander, leader) or *archegos* (captain, leader, chief, prince) is mistakenly used instead of *kephale*. For example in Ephesians 1.22-23, the writer uses the term *kephale* and not *archon* or *archegos* to show Christ as the Source and Supplier of God's Life . In I Corinthians 11.3, Paul uses kephale again to explain the creational relationship. This verse could read as follows:

> *But I want you to know that the source of every man is Christ; the source of woman, man; and the source of Christ, God.*

The same use of the word *kephale* is also used in Colossians 1.18-23 and 2.10,19 to reveal Christ as the Source of the body of believers.

Another issue that can potentially bring clarity concerning the priesthood is female submission. The English word "submit" is commonly translated from the Greek word *hupotasso* in the New Testament. When the word is used by Paul in I Corinthians 1:14, it means, "to show responsible behavior toward others."[4] In Ephesians 5.22-23, Paul uses *hupotasso* to mean "to add or unite one person or thing with another."[5] The wife is to identify with her husband even as believers identify with Christ. He asks the children and slaves to obey (*hupakouo*). And contrary to Greco-Roman culture, Paul asks the husband to love (*agape*) his wife. He instructs the husband to submit (*hupotasso*) to his wife (v.21).

The idea of a mutual respect and identification between the man and woman is encouraged by Paul (I Cor. 7.3-4; Gal. 5.13; Phil. 2.3; and I Pet .3.7). Patriarchy and a unilateral authority of the man over the woman are foreign to the Christian marriage relationship.

From a practical standpoint, there are several suggestions to be offered to help implement the concept explored here. The government of a home is a matter of the private decision of the husband and wife. They may choose to recognize the gifts and talents of each other and to utilize them appropriately. Mutual submission should be practiced by acknowledging the privilege of expression of the man and the woman. And if the husband or the wife chooses to recognize each other as the mouthpiece or spokesperson for the family, let such recognition be in the full understanding that the entire redeemed household is a royal priesthood.

Chapter Thirteen Endnotes

[1]C. H. Dodd, *The Bible Today* (Cambridge: University Press, 1952), p. 98.

[2]J. B. Lightfoot, *Saint Paul's Epistle to the Philippians* (New York: The MacMillan Company, 1900), p. 182-183.

[3]Berkeley and Alvera Mickelsen, "The 'Head' of the Epistles," *Christianity Today* (20 February 1981): 20.

[4]Susan C. Hyatt, *In The Spirit We're Equal: The Spirit, The Bible, and Women, A Revival Perspective* (Dallas: Hyatt Press, 1998) p.256 .

[5]Ibid.

.
.
.
.
. 13

FREQUENTLY ASKED QUESTIONS

There are some critical questions consistently encountered whenever we deal with the issue of co-laborship of men and women in ministry.

1. Can a woman be the senior elder in a local congregation of men and women?

2. How can a woman be ordained a bishop when the Scriptures state that a woman is to be submitted to a man?

3. If women are co-equal and co-substantial with men, will this not disrupt the order of the home?

4. Do the scriptures actually state that the man is the head of the household and, therefore, the priest of the home?

5. Should not the husband have the final word when there is a dispute or disagreement with the wife?

6. Is not male leadership the norm in the Scriptures since God is spoken of as Father, Jesus is a man, and the twelve disciples were all males?

7.   Were not all the apostles men?

8.   Is there a suggested way to transition the leader of a male-dominated ministry into one where women share in the leadership as elders?

9.   Are women emotionally capable of a senior leadership position? What about their mood swings and unpredictable behavior patterns?

We will address these questions briefly:

1. Can a woman be the chief elder in a local congregation of men and women?

The Scriptural references commonly used to establish an answer are: I Timothy 2:8-15, 3:1-7; Titus 1:5-11; and I Corinthians 11:2-16, 14:34-37.

a.   Male and female were both equally made in the image of God and bear the divine imprint of rationality, creativity, dominion, and righteousness.

b.   The commission to be fruitful, multiply, and exercise dominion was given to both the man and the woman.

c.   No indication is mentioned of male dominion over the woman.

The second epistle of John refers to the "elect lady and her children" which possibly is a house church with a female leader. A woman can teach and rule in a local congregation of men and women if she is received. The issue of "usurping authority" can apply to anyone, including a man, who attempts to take something that is not given. Women being "silent in the church" must obviously be put in proper context for there were women who did prophesy (Acts 2:17, 21:9).

The exclusion of women as bishop using the text that a bishop must be "husband of one wife" does not explicitly declare that a woman cannot be a bishop. It simply addresses the qualifications of a man who desires the office and corrected the issue of a multiplicity of wives or the issue of divorce, which obviously was not a problem among the women. And of course, submission is a mutual practice exercised by the man and the woman toward each other (I Cor. 7:3-4). The issue of "obedience" is never related to the woman but rather to the children in relation to their parents (Eph. 6:1).

2. Can a woman be ordained a bishop?

The challenge here rests in the passages of I Timothy 3:2 and Titus 1:6. The context of these references relates to a societal problem of multiplicity of wives or the frequency of divorce among men. Traditionally in Hebrew culture, it was the man that had the right to put away his wife. There were no such privileges given to the women. These references do not specifically declare that a woman cannot be a bishop, but address the qualification of <u>male candidates</u> possessing relational problems that were not common among the women. Of course, history reveals that there were notable women bishops (Theodora; see Dorothy Irvin, "The Ministry of Women in the Early Church: The Archaeological Evidence," Duke Divinity School Review no. 2 (1980): 76-86. See also Joan Morris, "The Lady Was a Bishop: The Hidden History of Women with Clerical Ordination and the Jurisdiction of Bishops" (New York: Macmillan, 1973).

3. If men and women are co-equal and co-substantial, will this disrupt the order of the home?

Intellectual ability is not limited to men. Women have demonstrated tremendous ability to manage the affairs of home, market place, and government. The issue here relates to the government of a local household. Each married couple needs to assess the abilities of each other and decide how best to divide the labor. This should not simply be a gender issue, but a performance level issue: who is best at doing what needs to be done . Today, the average household is already "disrupted" with both parents working outside of the home and both husband and wife sharing equally in the necessary chores including cooking, parenting, and managing. Such egalitarian relationships seem to survive as well or better than the male dominated models. Each couple needs to decide what is "disruptive;" and how to accomplish together their goals.

4. Is the man the head of the household and the priest of the home according to the Scriptures?

The Old Testament model of priest has been transferred to the New Testament erroneously. In the Old Testament (Num. 8:24-25), the priesthood was gender-specific (only males), tribal-specific (Levi), and age-specific (from age twenty-five to the age of fifty). In the New Testament, these specifications are eliminated, and a modified model of a universal priesthood evolves (I Pet. 2:5-9; Rev. 1:6, 5:10, 20:6). The Old Testament model of priest with its sacerdotal responsibilities have been erroneously transferred to the male head of household who is supposed to serve as the mediator or the representative of the family before God. This concept excludes the redemptive equality of all believers to offer spiritual sacrifices of thanksgiving, prayers, and intercessions on their own behalf. There is indeed, a new priesthood. And conceivably, each redeemed member of a household is a priest with Jesus Christ being the only high priest and the only mediator between humanity and God. Yes, the man can be the spokesman for the family if the individual family chooses. However, there is no Scriptural validation for a New Testament priesthood without the above mentioned modifications.

5. Should the husband have the final word when there is a disagreement with the wife?

Once again, the issue is not a gender matter, but an issue of ethics, morality, and correctness. When there is a disagreement between a husband and wife, the issue of gender is not the determining factor but the correctness of the position taken. Both of them may be correct. Rather than enforcing a gender right to have the last word, it may be advisable to consider delaying some action on the matter under discussion. If the Scriptural references to "silence" or "submission" only applies to the woman in these matters of a domestic dispute, then valuable counsel may be nullified simply because of a male-dominated position. It is advisable that the man and the woman honor a position of mutual respect.

6. Do not the Scripture indicate patriarchy since God is referred to as Father, Jesus is a man, and the original twelve disciples were all males?

This argument seems practical except when you apply the principle to the 12 disciples. Notice that none of the original disciples were Gentiles. Should the absence of Gentiles among the disciples or the fact that Jesus was a Jew be the basis for excluding Gentiles from salvation? The answer is obvious. God is a spirit and efforts to designate gender are not Scriptural. The concept of God as Father is a revelation of the caring relationship that exists with the created order. To call God Mother causes no violence to God, nor does it disempower God.

7. Were not all the apostles men?

The original twelve were all men. However, if the apostolic requirements were to have seen the Lord, witnessed the resurrection, and to have been commissioned by the Lord, then Mary Magdalene was the first apostle to the apostles (Matt. 28:1-10). The epistle to the Romans record that Junia, a woman, was noted among the apostles (16:7). In fact, Tabitha was specifically referred to as a certain disciple (Acts 9:36).

8. Is there a way to transition a male-dominated leadership model into a plural-leadership model of co-laborship between men and women?

Teaching and instruction should precede any deliberate action. The requirements for women and men should be equitable. Gradual changes are at times more profitable than revolutionary ones. However, too much delay in the process will defeat the purpose. There should be allowances for emotional responses from the congregation and even from among the elders. Some of the greatest resistance will come from women themselves. If the elders sit on the platform during regular services, it would be advisable to immediately seat the female elders there also. Begin to open up opportunities for the women to participate in the public services. Gradually phase out the designation of meetings restricted just to women or men exclusively, since these will continue to breed division. Instruct the women to preach, teach, and behave themselves like women and not emulate the men in their mannerism or public behavior.

9. Are women emotionally capable of senior leadership? Are they not subject to mood swings and unpredictable behavioral patterns that could prove detrimental?

The answer to this question can be more effectively addressed in the section entitled Gender, Religion, and Science.

Bibliography

Aburdene, Patricia and John Naisbitt. *Megatrends for Women: From Liberation To Leadership*. New York: Ballantine Books, 1992.

Agonito, Rosemary. *History of Ideas on Woman*. New York: Berkley Publishing Group, 1977.

Allport, Gordon W. *The Nature of Prejudice*. New York: Addison-Wesley Publishing Company, 1979.

Astin, Helen S. *The Woman Doctorate in America*. New York: Russell Sage Foundation, 1969.

Barish, David P. *Sociobiology and Behavior*. New York: Elsevier, 1977.

Bellis, Alice Ogden. *Helpmates, Harlots and Heroes: Women's Stories in the Hebrew Bible*. Louisville: Westminister/John Knox Press, 1994.

Bilizekian, Gilbert. *Beyond Sex Roles: A Guide for the Study of Female Sex Roles in the Bible*. Grand Rapids: Baker Book House, 1985.

Bird, Phyllis. *Images of Women in the Old Testament, in Religion and Sexism: Images of Women in the Jewish and Christian Tradition, ed. R. Reuther*. New York: Simon and Schuster, 1974.

Bristow, John Temple. *What Paul Really Said About Women*. San Francisco: Harper & Row, 1988.

Bushnell, Katherine. *God's Word to Women: One Hundred Bible Studies on Woman's Place In The Divine Economy*. North Collins, N.Y.: Ray Munson, 1923.

Clouse, Bonnidell and Robert G. Clouse. *Women in Ministry*. Downers Grove: Intervarsity Press, 1989.

Cole, Jonathan. *Fair Science: Women in the Scientific Community*. New York: Free Press, 1979.

Coleman, James. *Community Conflict*. Glencoe, Il.: Free Press, 1957.

Cross, F.L. *The Oxford Dictionary of the Christian Church*. London: Oxford University Press, 1974.

Davis, J.M. *Dictionary of the Bible*. Grand Rapids: Baker Book House, 1972.

Dodd, C.H. *The Bible Today*. Cambridge: University Press, 1952.

Ellicott, C.J. *An Old Testament Commentary for English Readers*. London: Cassell and Company, 1901.

Epstein, Cynthia Fuchs. *Woman's Place: Options and Limits in Professional Careers*. Berkeley: University of California Press, 1970.

Epstein, Cynthia Fuchs. *Women in Law*. New York: basic Books, 1981.

Feathers, Frank. *Reinventing the World*. Toronto: Summerhill Press, 1989.

Fiorenza, Elisabeth Schussler. *In Memory of Her: A Feminist Theological Reconstruction of Christian Origins*. New York: Crossroad, 1989.

Fisher, G.P. *History of Christian Doctrine*. Edinburg: T & T Clark, 1927.

Freeman, James M. *Manners and Customs of the Bible*. Plainfield: Logos International, 1972.

Geschwind, Norman. "Language of the Brain," *Scientific America* 241 (3), 1979.

Goddman, Erving. *Gender Advertisements*. London: Macmillan, 1976.

Goldberg, Steven. *The Inevitability of Patriarchy*, 2d ed. New York: Morrow, 1974.

Gonzalez, Justo. *The Story of Christianity*. San Francisco: Harper, 1984.

Gould, Stephen J. *The Measure of Man*. New York: Norton, 1981.

Grenz, Stanley J. *Women in the Church*. Downers Grove: InterVarsity Press, 1995.

Grimm, Harold. *The Reformation Era*. New York: Macmillan Publishing, 1973.

Gundry, Patricia. *Neither Slave Nor Free*. New York: Harper & Row, 1987.

Gundry, Patricia. *Woman Be Free!* Grand Rapids: Zondervan, 1977.
Gundry, Patricia. *Heirs Together: Mutual Submission in Marriage*. Grand Rapids: Zondervan, 1980.

Hastings, James. *Dictionary of the Apostolic Church*. Edinburg: T & L Clark, 1926.

Hochschild, Arlie. *Changing Women in a Changing Soceity*. Chicago: University of Chicago Press, 1973.

Howe, Margaret E. *Women and Church Leadership*. Grand Rapids: Zondervan, 1992.

Hull, Gretchen Baebelein. *Equal to Serve*. Grand Rapids: Baker Books, 1991.

Hyatt, Susan C. *In The Spirit We're Equal: The Spirit, The Bible, and Women, A Revival Perspective*. Dallas: Hyatt Press, 1998.

Kirkpatrick, Jean. *Political Women*. New York: Basic Books, 1974.

Kramer, Ross Shepherd. *Her Share of the Blessing*. New York: Oxford University Press, 1992.

Kroeger, Catherine Clark and James R. Beck, eds. *Women, Abuse, and the Bible*. Grand Rapids: Baker Books, 1996.

Kroeger, Catherine Clark, Mary Evans and Elaine Storkey. *Study Bible For Women*. Grand Rapids: Baker Books, 1995.

Kroeger, Richard Clark and Catherine Clark Kroeger. *I Suffer Not a Woman: Rethinking I Timothy 2:11-15 in Light of Ancient Evidence*. Grand Rapids: Baker Books, 1992.

Lamsa, George M. *New Testament Commentary*. Philadelphia: A.J. Holman, 1945.

Lamsa, George M. *Old Testament Light*. Philadelphia: A.J. Holman, 1945.

Latourette, Kenneth Scott. *A History of Christianity, Volume 1*. New York: Harper and Row, 1975.

Lazardeld, Paul F. And Morris Rosenberg, eds. *Language of Social Research: A Reader in the Methodolgy of Social Research*. Glencoe, Ill.: Free Press, 1955

Lewontin, R.C. Steven Rose and Leon Kamin. *Not in Our Genes*. New York: Basic Books, 1973.

Lightfoot, J.B. *Saint Paul's Epistle to the Philippians*. New York: MacMillan, 1900.

Lockyer, Herbert. *All the Women of the Bible*. Grand Rapids: Zondervan, 1967.

Luther, Martin Luther. *A Commentary on St. Paul's Epistle to the Galatians*. London: James Clark and Co., 1953.

Maccoby, Eleanor E. And Carol N. Jacklin. *The Psychology of Sex Differences*. Stanford, Ca.: Stanford University Press, 1974.

Mayers, Marvin K. *Christianity Confronts Culture*. Grand Rapids: Zondervan, 1987.

Mickelsen, Alvera, ed. *Women, Authority and the Bible*. Downers Grove: Intervarsity Press, 1086.

Murray, Henry A. And Clyde Kluckholm. *Personality in Nature, Society and Culture.*

New York:Alfred A. Knopf, 1950.

Neusner, Jacob. *The Mishnah*. Philadelphia: Trinity Press, 1992.

Newson, Carol A. And Sharon H. Ringe. *The Women's Bible Commentary*. Louisville: Westminister/John Knox Press, 1992.

Osborn, Daisy Washburn. *Creation Realities*. Tulsa: International Gospel Center, 1988.

Osborn, Daisy Washburn. *Old Testament Discoveries*. Tulsa: International Gospel Center, 1988.

Parson, Talcott. *The Family: Its Function and Destiny*. New York: Harper & Row, 1949.

Pfitzner, Victor C. *Paul and the Agon Motif: Traditional Athletic Imagery in the Pauline Literature*. Leiden: Brill, 1967.

Pillai, K.C. *Light Through An Eastern Window*. New York: Robert Speller & Sons, 1963.

Piper, John and Wayne Gruden, eds. *Recovering Biblical Manhood and Womanhood: A Reponse to Evangelical Feminism*. Wheaton, Ill.: Crossway, 1991.

Reskin, Barbara F. *Sex Segregation in the Workplace: Trends, Explanations and Remedies*. Washington: National Academy Press, 1984.

Reskin, Barbara F. And Heidi Hartmann. *Women's Work, Men's Work: Sex Segregation in the Job*. Washington: National Academy Press, 1986.

Ruether, Rosemary Radford. *Women and Redemption: A Theological History*. Minneapolis: Fortress Press, 1998.

Ruether, Rosemary Radford. *Woman Guides: Readings Toward a Feminist Theology*. Boston: Beacon Press, 1996.

Sherman, Julia A. *On the Psychology of Women: A Survey of Empirical Studies*. Springfield, Il.: Charles C. Thomas, 1971.

Snyder, Howard. *Earth Currents*. Nashville: Abingdon Press, 1995.

Spake, Kluame Simonds. *You Are Acceptable To Me*.

Spake, Kluame Simonds. *From Enmity to Equality*. Suwanee, Ga.: Workforce Press, 1994.

Starr, Lee Ann. *The Bible Status of Woman*. Zarephath, N.J.: Pillar of Fire, 1955.

Swidler, Leonard. *Biblical Affirmation of Women*. Philadelphia: Westminister Press, 1979.

Trojesia, Karen Jo. *When Women Were Priests: Women's Leadership in the Early Church and the Scandal of Their Subordination in the Rise of Christianity.* San Francisco: Harper and Row, 1993.

Trombley, Charles. *Who Said Women Can't Teach.* Plainfield, N.J.: Logos International, 1989.

Tucker, Ruth and Walter Liefeld. *Daughters of the Church: Women and Ministry From New Testament Times to the Present.* Grand Rapids: Zondervan, 1986.

Wegner, Judith Romney. *Chattel or Person?* New York: Oxford University Press, 1988.

Willis, John R. *A History of Christian Thought.* New York: Exposition Press, 1976.

Wilson, Edward O. *Sociobiology: The New Synthesis.* Cambridge: Belknap Press of Harvard University Press, 1975.

Wright, Fred. *Manners and Customs of Bible Lands.* Chicago: Moody Press, 1953.

Wylie, Phillip. *Generation of Vipers.* New York: Farrar, Rinehart, 1942.

Dr. Kirby and Sandra Clements

Dr. Kirby and Sandra Clements have served as associate Pastors to Archbishop Earl Paulk at the 10,000-member Cathedral of the Holy Spirit since 1979. In 1997 Dr. Kirby was ordained as Canon Missioner and in 1999 installed as Bishop of the Harvester of Network of Churches.

They travel extensively, representing the office of the Archbishop, both nationally and internationally, and have co-authored several books.

Other Publications

A Philosophy of Ministry
The Second
Discernment

Make all inquiries to the following addresses, phone numbers, email addresses.

Cathedral Shoppe, Cathedral of the Holy Spirit
4650 Flat Shoals Parkway, Decatur, GA 30034
network@randomc.com; cathedral@randomc.com
404-243-5020

Clements Family Ministries
3310 Harvester Woods Road, Suite A, Decatur, GA 30034
404-288-0981 or Email:sachcl@aol.com